Sharankumar Limbale, one of M
writer-activists, is the author of sev
about Dalit life. He has also edite
criticism and the history of the Dalit movement. Limbale's most recent
works are *Upalya* and *Hindu*, novels about Dalit politics. His
groundbreaking autobiographical work, *Akkarmashi*, has recently
appeared in English as *The Outcaste*. Limbale has received numerous
honours and awards for his contribution to Dalit literature and the
Dalit movement. Limbale is a member of the faculty of the
Yashwantrao Chavan Maharashtra Open University, Nashik. He and
his wife, Kusum, and their three children live in Pune.

Alok Mukherjee teaches about Indian culture and society at York
University in Toronto, Canada. He has recently completed a critical
examination of the rise and present status of English Studies in India,
*'This Gift of English': English Education and the Formation of Alternative
Hegemonies in India*. Mukherjee is a human rights activist and a former
chief commissioner of the Human Rights Commission for the province
of Ontario, and has written extensively on human rights and equity.
He is married to Arun Prabha Mukherjee, a well-known literary critic,
and has a son.

Towards an Aesthetic of Dalit Literature
HISTORY, CONTROVERSIES AND CONSIDERATIONS

Sharankumar Limbale

Translated and edited,
with a commentary,
by
Alok Mukherjee

Orient Longman

ORIENT LONGMAN PRIVATE LIMITED

Registered Office
3-6-752 Himayatnagar, Hyderabad 500 029 (A.P.), India
e-mail: hyd2_orlongco@sancharnet.in

Other Offices
Bangalore, Bhopal, Bhubaneshwar, Chandigarh, Chennai, Ernakulam,
Guwahati, Hyderabad, Jaipur, Kolkata, Lucknow, Mumbai,
New Delhi, Patna

© Orient Longman Private Limited 2004
First English Edition 2004
First Marathi Edition 1996
Marathi: Sharankumar Limbale
English Translation: Alok Kumar Mukherjee
Originally published in Marathi as *Dalit Sahityache Saundaryashastra*,
by Arun Kamble, Kanta Prakashan

ISBN 81 250 2656 8

Typeset by
Scribe Consultants
New Delhi

Printed in India at
Baba Barkha Nath Printers
New Delhi

Published by
Orient Longman Private Limited
1/24 Asaf Ali Road
New Delhi 110 002
e-mail: olldel@del6.vsnl.net.in

Contents

Content

Translator's Introduction

What is Dalit literature? What are its concerns and features? What aesthetic considerations should be taken into account in interpreting Dalit writing? Is it appropriate to apply to Dalit literature the criteria commonly used in assessing the work of non-Dalit writers generally, and upper caste Hindu writers in particular? Who is a Dalit, anyway? These are among the questions that Sharankumar Limbale explores in his book *Dalit Sahityache Saundaryashastra*. First published in Marathi in 1996, Limbale's book is a wide-ranging exploration by a Dalit writer, of the history, controversies and considerations pertaining to the emerging literature of Dalits.

Since most Dalit writing, and discussion of this writing, have been in the various regional languages of India, very little of either is accessible in English. This is a major gap, given that much of the theorizing in India and abroad about Indian literatures, culture and society, whether from Marxist, postcolonial or subaltern perspectives, has been in English. Only some of the theorists have drawn on materials from the regional languages, and even they have taken virtually no note of interventions by Dalits. Discussion of the literary and cultural representations of marginalized and dispossessed people, such as members of India's untouchable and aboriginal communities, has, for the most part, been based on the writings of upper caste writers, such as Mulk Raj Anand, Mahasweta Devi and Premchand. For Dalit writers, many of these narratives are part of a 'discourse of pity'.

Dalits are an important political and social force in India. Their literary and critical writings constitute a major challenge to, and questioning of, the theorizing about Indian politics, society, culture and literature by intellectuals from upper caste Hindu and other dominant communities, and by non-Indians. To fail to pay attention to this challenge and questioning, is to engage in a hegemonic discourse that excludes the realities and experiences of nearly a quarter of the country's people.

As a small effort to fill this gap, I have translated Limbale's book. Eleanor Zelliot notes in her forthcoming essay, 'The Birth of Dalit Literature in Maharashtra,' that until the publication of this translation, Aniket Jaaware's 'Eating, and Eating with, the Dalit: A Re-consideration Touching upon Marathi Poetry' remains 'the only literary criticism [in English] from within the Dalit community'.

Sharankumar Limbale, a pre-eminent contemporary Dalit writer in Marathi and Hindi, came to prominence with the publication of *Akkarmashi*, his autobiographical narrative of rural Dalit life. Originally written in Marathi, it became available to a wider audience when the Hindi translation appeared in 1991. (The English translation, *The Outcaste*, was made available in 2003.)

Though Limbale's book is concerned primarily with the evolution and features of Dalit literature in Marathi, the conclusions he draws and the case that he makes regarding the distinct purpose, politics and poetics of Dalit literature have wider relevance. Limbale argues that Dalit literature is unique, even though its evolution may be seen in the context of the history of various regional literatures—Marathi, in his own case.

Dalit Sahityache Saundaryashastra is a response. Dalit writers have insisted that their writing has a particular purpose and audience, that these have an important bearing on their literary/aesthetic decisions, and that, therefore, their work should not be assessed by 'universal' criteria, which, in India, carry the markers of caste and class. This has led to a rather heated reaction from upper caste literary critics, as a review of the debate in the pages of just one Hindi literary publication, *Hans*, shows.

Dalit writing has been accused of lacking in literary merit when measured against universal criteria. Dalit writers have been charged with being divisive and sectarian, using disrespectful and offensive language towards Hindu divinities and revered figures, and engaging in distortions of pre- and post-independence Indian history. It has been suggested that some Dalits were treating literature as simply another arena of affirmative action, and were claiming to be writers even though they did not have the ability to write.[1]

Limbale's book is dialogically related to these critiques and questionings, insofar as dialogism, according to Bakhtin,[2] involves conflict. Limbale asserts that Dalit literature is distinct. He points out that Dalit reality is a liminal reality in time and space. The content and form of the literature that is about this liminality has its own particular features. In identifying these particularities, the book talks back to the universalist assertions of India's dominant-group literary theorists. Limbale's rejection of the hegemony of the caste-based universal challenges the neat binary world of postcolonial literary theory by calling attention to the internal contradictions of Indian society.

Limbale is not the only Dalit writer to have written on the form and purpose of Dalit literature. As the body of this literature grows, the subject has begun to receive considerable attention. I have chosen to translate this book because it is so comprehensive—it locates Dalit literature within a historical context, foregrounds its ideological concerns, and identifies its literary and aesthetic characteristics in a way that few other writings on the subject do.

This translation begins with an essay, 'Reading Sharankumar

---

1. See for example, Bhavdev Pandey, 'Hindi Sahitya kaa Savarna Itihaas: Nahin, Yeh Jaativad Nahin Hai' ('Caste History of Hindi Literature: No, This is Not Casteism'); Namwar Singh, quoted in Roopchand Gautam, 'Dalit Sahitya Par Aur Bhi Bahas Jaroori Hai' ('Further Debate about Dalit Literature is Essential'); Hetu Bharadwaj, 'Ghaatak Nahin Hogaa Sahitya kaa Yeh Vibhaajan?' ('Won't This Division of Literature be Fatal?'); and Shailendra Kumar Tripathi, 'Dalit Chintan Banaam Itihaas' ('Dalit Thinking versus History'). For a comprehensive survey of the upper caste Hindu critics' objections to Dalit writing and Dalit thinking, see Arun Mukherjee, 'The Emergence of Dalit Writing' and 'Facing the Interrogations of Dalit Writing,' in *Postcolonialism: My Living*, 41–51, 52–64.

2. See, for example, Bakhtin, 'Discourse on the Novel,' in M M Bakhtin, *The Dialogic Imagination: Four Essays*, 259–422; and Ken Hirschkop, 'Is Dialogism for Real?'

Limbale's *Towards an Aesthetic of Dalit Literature:* From Erasure to Assertion,' in which I have provided a commentary on some of the key historical and theoretical issues raised by Limbale. The next six chapters contain the translation of Limbale's Marathi text. In the first of these chapters, Limbale questions the triadic concept of 'satyam' (the true), 'shivam' (the sacred) and 'sundaram' (the beautiful). He turns the concept, which is the foundation of traditional Hindu aesthetics, on its head in terms of its applicability to Dalit experience. This is followed by 'Dalit Literature: Form and Purpose,' in which Limbale provides an overview of the considerations relevant to the form and purpose of Dalit literature. The chapter also situates Marathi Dalit literature within the historical context of Marathi literature. The next three chapters examine the various debates and controversies surrounding Dalit literature in relation to Ambedkarism, Marxism and African American literature respectively. Following these, in 'Dalit Literature and Aesthetics,' Limbale proposes a framework for reading and evaluating Dalit literature. The last chapter reproduces an extended interview that I conducted, with Limbale, over two days in May 2001. In this conversation, Limbale speaks frankly and provocatively on a wide range of issues, questions and challenges Dalit literature and the Dalit movement face today. The book thus addresses both the historical and the theoretical aspects of Dalit aesthetics.

I would like to say a few words about my translation. As may be expected, Marathi has its own linguistic, grammatical, syntactic and rhetorical peculiarities, which are not fully translatable. My objective here has been to seek ease of reading over a mechanical fidelity. This has meant that at certain places I have preferred to interpret—to convey the sense of a statement—rather than translate the words literally. To further aid the reading of the book, I have provided a glossary of words, concepts and allusions that may not be readily understood by, or be widely known to non-Marathi readers.

For those interested in extending their acquaintance with Dalit literature, I have included a select list of works by Dalit writers from various Indian languages.

Acknowledgements

I owe a huge debt of gratitude to Arun Prabha Mukherjee, my wife. Her work introduced me to Dalit literature and made me think about the profound issues raised by this literature in a broader context of the role of literature in the struggle for human rights, equity and social justice. The title of this translation is partly an echo of that of one of her early books, *Towards an Aesthetic of Opposition*.

Ato Sekyi-Otu, professor of social and political thought and a leading Frantz Fanon expert, and Janine Ayesha Willie from the Tsawataineuk First Nation in British Columbia and a considerable scholar of Native Canadian Literatures, are two colleagues and friends to whom I owe special thanks. Over a period of nearly two years at York University, the three of us read and compared works by Canada's Mixed Blood People of First Nations Origins (popularly known as the Metis) and by Dalit writers. This was an invaluable experience in terms of looking at literature from an entirely new perspective.

Ramnika Gupta and Ramesh Warkhede made helpful comments on parts of the translation and my commentary, as did Ato. I would like to thank them.

While working on the translation, I had the privilege of conversations with a number of Dalit writers and critics. It is not possible to name them all, but I do wish to place on record my appreciation of the readiness with which Ramnath Chavan, Laxman Gaikwad, Manohar Jadhav, Jyoti Lanjewar and Dr Gangadhar Pantawane, the elder statesman of Dalit literature, shared their insights and issues with me. Many of them took me into their homes, and I cherish their friendship.

It has been a joy and an education to collaborate with Sharankumar Limbale. He and his wife, Kusum, welcomed me in their home and made me feel like a member of the family.

Limbale embodies what he means by the term writer-activist. Working with him on this translation, understanding the context in which he wrote the book, finding the words until he was satisfied that they were the right ones for what he wanted to say, have made this project a profound experience for me.

It has been a pleasure to work with Sivapriya, my editor at Orient Longman. Her reading of the translation has been critical, and at the same time, sensitive. I thank her for her help in producing a text that is considerably superior to the original she received from me!

Meenakshi Mukherjee, one of India's best literary critics and mentor to many, as well as Nandini Rao and Hemlata Shankar took a keen interest in the publication of this translation. I thank them for believing in its worth.

ALOK MUKHERJEE
York University
Toronto, Canada

1

Reading Sharankumar Limbale's *Towards an Aesthetic of Dalit Literature:* From Erasure to Assertion

ALOK MUKHERJEE

Indian literary history and theory, as well as the teaching of Indian literatures, are spectacularly silent about Dalit literature. Yet, Dalit cultural and critical productions make a significant critical intervention in the thinking and writing about Indian society, history, culture and literature. Babasaheb Ambedkar – and Mahatma Jotirao Phule, who influenced him greatly – interrogated the dominant, casteist constructions of Indian identity. Through his examinations of Indian history, mythology and the sacred texts of Hinduism, Ambedkar made a powerful case for a distinct Dalit identity. His work enabled future generations of Dalits to assert themselves as subjects through political activism, organizing, and literary and critical writing. Inspired by the work of Ambedkar, writers like Limbale have produced an important body of literature that narrates Dalit reality and experience.

Arjun Dangle, the Marathi Dalit writer, editor and activist, says, 'Dalit literature is marked by revolt and negativism, since it is closely associated with the hopes for freedom by a group of people who, as untouchables, are victims of social, economic and cultural inequality.' Dangle traces the origin of Dalit literature to Ambedkar. 'His revolutionary ideas stirred into action all the Dalits of Maharashtra and gave them a new self-respect. Dalit literature is nothing but the literary expression of this awareness.' By the 1970s, a sufficient corpus of Dalit literature had developed so that, according to Dangle, 'thinking Dalit critics began to theorize on Dalit literature and its role.'

> Dalit literature is not simply literature ... Dalit literature is associated with a movement to bring about change ... At the very first glance, it will be strongly evident that there is no established critical theory or point of view behind them [i.e. Dalit writings]; instead, there is new thinking and a new point of view. (Dangle 1994, vii–viii)

Dalit writers' theorizing about the need, role, content and form of Dalit literature constitutes their answer to Gayatri Chakravorty Spivak's now-famous question, 'Can the subaltern speak?'

Spivak posed the question with reference to the colonizer—colonized framework within which much of the theorizing about postcoloniality and subalternity emanating from Indian and metropolitan intellectual circles has taken place. A work such as Limbale's is a subversive move: it explodes this binary and exposes the inner contradictions that it conceals.

Limbale establishes the Dalits' subalternity not in a colonial structure, but in the caste-based social, cultural and economic structure of Hindu society. Here, the village becomes the metropolis, and Dalits exist literally on the periphery. Dalit settlements are not only apart from the upper caste Hindu settlements, they are actually outside the boundary of the village. This physical segregation signifies other separations. Dalits do the work, live the life, eat the food and wear the garment that the upper caste Hindu will not. They draw water from a separate well, and cremate their dead in a separate space. Dalits are the upper caste Hindu's Other. But this Other is not only separate and different, like the member of another ethno-cultural, religious or linguistic group. This Other is a part of Hindu society, and yet apart from it. Inscribed in that apartness and difference is inferiority. Dalits occupy the lowest place in the Hindu hierarchical order.

The inferior location of Dalits is not only spatial it is also normative. The Dalit is untouchable. The play of desire and revulsion works here in a very particular way. The work of the Dalits is essential for maintaining the upper caste Hindu's purity. If they did not clean latrines, skin dead animals, and remove the carcasses, the social life of the upper caste will be unclean, polluted and diseased. And yet, just as these are revolting activities, so is the Dalit an object of revulsion, precisely for doing them, even though it is the upper caste Hindu who forces Dalits into carrying them out. Dalits enable the purity of upper caste society, and become impure in the process. This society needs the Dalits' labour, indeed, depends on it for its elegant survival, but does not wish to be reminded of it. Scriptural authority was invoked to designate the Dalit as polluted and untouchable. Even the shadow of this Other was to be avoided. The upper caste Hindu's obsessive preoccupation with purity and cleanliness, and the relationship of desire and revulsion that it produced, can, no doubt, be read in terms of the popular psychological framework of desire and taboo, utilized by postcolonial theorists such as Fanon, Homi Bhabha and Robert Young.[1] Here, we are concerned with the social, cultural and political dimensions of this relationship.

The shape and nature of the Dalit's subalternity, then, are quite unlike those produced by colonial relations. The Dalit's subaltern status is inherited from birth and sanctioned by sacred authority. It is eternal and unalterable.

This peculiar social condition of Dalits, indispensable to the reproduction of social life yet invisible in it, is mirrored in the realm of culture. The history of Marathi literature as narrated by Limbale shows how the alterity of this subaltern has been replicated in culture to ensure that Dalits will not have voice or, for a long time, presence. Early Marathi literature, written during the high tide of Brahmanism, was absorbed in what Limbale calls 'the binaries of desire and freedom from desire'. There was no place for Dalits in the content of this literature.

---

1. See, for example, Frantz Fanon, *Black Skin, White Masks*; Homi K Bhabha, *The Location of Culture*; and Robert J C Young, *Colonial Desire: Hybridity in Theory, Culture and Race*.

The space that they occupied outside the village in real life was erased in the world of literature. Thus, if society ensured its purity by relegating the untouchable to a liminal space, literature went a step further. It ensured that the untouchable would not pollute its world even by touching that space.

In Limbale's telling, upper caste Hindu society was not content with avoiding the Dalit in its literature. It also made sure that Dalits could not speak in the tongue of the upper caste. Having determined that Dalits were impure and polluted, it legislated that they were not to learn or read Sanskrit, the language of the gods and, so, the ultimate trope of Brahmanism.

It would appear that the upper caste Hindus achieved in literature what they could not in real life, namely, a complete silencing, if not erasure, of the untouchable Other with no chance of being polluted by the untouchable's shadow. This erasure was not confined to the literature and culture of Maharashtra alone. A review of Indian literary history would show that the untouchable was absent from Sanskrit and other regional literatures as well. For example, of three randomly picked collections of essays on Indian literatures and culture written over twenty years, only one – Hogan and Pandit's *Literary India* – contains one essay dealing with caste, and that too, in a modern novel, Rabindranath Tagore's *Gora*.[2] The untouchable Other simply had been written out of existence.

Limbale, however, seems to suggest that this was more a wish fulfillment than an accomplished fact. Limbale's invocation of Kabir as one of the originary figures of the Dalit tradition suggests that there were, in fact, people from the lowest ranks of the caste system who were making literature. They did not write in the high languages of the society, but in the vernacular of the common people. The power and impact of their work were such that those whom Limbale calls 'the high priests of literature'

---

2. The three collections are: A Poddar, ed., *Indian Literature: Proceedings of a Seminar*; Ramvilas Sharma, *Paramparaa kaa Mulyankan*; and Patrick Colm Hogan and Lalita Pandit, eds., *Literary India: Comparative Studies in Aesthetics, Colonialism, and Culture.*

could not ignore them. They were, or had to be, included in literary history. However, the particularity of the experience they were writing about, as well as the space they were writing from, were not acknowledged. They were normalized into the mainstream of Brahmanical literature, as oppositional voices or as reformers. Often, as products of their time, they too accepted the legitimacy of what Limbale describes as a preoccupation with 'serving at the feet of the soul and the supreme soul'.

That, we know, is one of the problematics associated with subaltern speech. Often, it appears to take on the voice of the master. But the important point is that Brahmanical literature could not wish away either the reality lurking at the edges of its pure, unpolluted space, or the inhabitants of those edges, the very beings who by their labour ensured this purity and freedom from pollution. Limbale uses the term 'reformist-liberalism' to describe the politics of Dalits' inclusion in the Brahmanical literature of what he calls modern and contemporary periods. In these periods, this literature moved from erasure to containment. Unable to imagine the untouchable Other out of existence, Brahmanical literature now sought to confine it within a discourse marked by 'sympathy' and 'compassion', to use Limbale's terms.

No doubt, this shift was as much the product of a changing social consciousness as of a political juncture. A variety of factors loosened the stranglehold of Brahmanism and feudalism. European colonialism, the establishment of an English public education system, the advent of industrial capitalism, the emergence of a bourgeoisie, the rise of a working class, contact with ideas of rationalism and Enlightenment, on the one hand, and a nationalist anti-colonial movement, which was accompanied by the recognition in certain liberal circles of the need for social reform, on the other, doubtless contributed to the shift in the mindset that Limbale alludes to. Of no less importance was the fact that Dalits themselves were no longer prepared to be silent occupants of the liminal space to which they had been confined for centuries. Leaders like Phule spoke out with persuasive force. Closer to our time, Ambedkar organized Dalits into a force to be contended with. Phule and Ambedkar used the full force of their erudition to take apart the procedures Brahmanism had used to maintain the casteist social order. And they complicated matters further by refusing to automatically embrace the nationalist anti-colonial movement. They were prepared to enter into strategic conversations with the colonial rulers for obtaining remedies for centuries of caste oppression. As far as Dalits were concerned, the savarna Hindu society, with its own record, could not now expect their automatic allegiance in its fight against the British.

Postcolonial thought, of whatever ideological hue, has found it difficult to come to terms with this two-pronged move. Indeed, during the independence movement and after, bourgeois nationalists as well as Marxists accused Dalit leaders of complicity with the colonial power, and Ambedkar, personally, of being a British agent. The following comments about him by S G Sardesai, a prominent Communist leader of the 1970s, made in the course of a reappraisal of the question of caste, reveal the fraught nature of upper caste Hindu response to the Dalits' struggle to alter their condition.

There were certain contradictions in his outlook, his views, his role in Indian politics, taken as a whole. He was very conscious that the 'untouchables' needed allies for their emancipation. He was conscious that it was the exploited, touchable mass of workers that was their natural ally. He made efforts to bring about such an alliance ... On the other hand, his deep and understandable bitterness against the ossified, suffocating hindu caste structure led him to denounce caste hindus in a generalised way (more particularly, in his mass agitation) and to rouse the 'untouchables' against all the rest ...

Similarly, he was a nationalist, and absolutely, in no sense, a British agent. At the same time, the tendency to consider the British as a 'third', and hence a disinterested power from whom he could expect sympathy and support against caste hindu dominations, was also there in him. This, again, was a characteristic and wholly understandable trait of all the mass leaders of the 'untouchables' and the shudras, up to Dr Ambedkar's time ...

Before the achievement of national independence, Indian nationalists, including the leftists in the national movement reacted only to the negative aspects of Dr Ambedkar's views and role. Generally, he was considered 'pro-British' and 'anti-national'. His positive role was ignored. Now, in recent years, the pendulum is swinging to the other extreme. The negative features of his role are often attempted to be explained away as the result of the shortcomings and weaknesses of the national movement, particularly of Mahatma Gandhi. The positive contribution of Mahatma Gandhi and other social reformers to the cause of the 'untouchables' is overlooked and sometimes, even denied. (Sardesai 1979, 40–41)

The ambiguity in Sardesai's evaluation of Ambedkar's role and views is revealing. That this is partly due to the Dalit leader's perceived failure to make common cause with the working class and his tendency to see all Hindus in 'a generalised way' is clear. The somewhat patronizing tone of the analysis also suggests that, while Sardesai may understand where Ambedkar was 'coming from', he does not think that Ambedkar was capable of knowing better. The Communist leader, himself a savarna Hindu, seems to be saying that while the centuries-old practice of untouchability spawned by the casteism of Hindu society was wrong, and Dalits were right to fight against it, they could not be allowed to map their own struggle. Gandhi's thinking, in fact, was even more problematic. During discussions with the British government regarding India's independence, he declared himself to be the real representative of the untouchables, denying Ambedkar's right to be the chosen representative.

Limbale points out that this duality becomes evident early in literature. Where early Marathi literature sought to erase Dalits completely, modern and contemporary writings followed a strategy of containment. The untouchable Other was now visible, but only in the context of a discourse of 'sympathy' and 'compassion'. Dalits were still not speaking subjects; they were not people with 'self-pride', as Limbale notes. This representation of Dalits as objects of pity, rather than as authors of their own stories was not confined to Marathi literature alone. Critics besides Limbale have been troubled by the treatment of Dalit characters in the writings of such prominent writers as Premchand and Mulk Raj Anand. In their view, these representations do not show Dalits as they are, but as helpless and child-like people who cannot make their own decisions or take action. In Anand's novel, *Untouchable*, for example, the protagonist, Bakha, instead of opting for radical action, submits to Gandhi's pacifism, and is thus contained (Mukherjee 1998, 143).

This is not, of course, what always happened in real life. As Sardesai's troubled commentary on Ambedkar suggests, Dalits charted their own course of action. Though consigned to the margins of society, and to the same tasks that kept the upper caste society pure and pollution-free, they became a visible presence, and their voices began to break through the boundaries that had kept them apart. But if they could no longer be kept out or erased, Brahmanical literature could certainly keep them in their place, and thus protect the purity of its space. It is these representations of Dalits by upper caste Hindu writers, rather than those created by Dalit writers themselves, which have been the basis of any discussion of issues of caste and casteism in literary history and theory. Thus, even a radical critic such as Gayatri Spivak, for example, has based her entire exploration of the life experiences of Adivasis or aboriginal communities, another group that has been kept outside the boundaries of the village, on the writings of the upper caste Bengali writer, Mahasweta Devi, several of whose works Spivak has translated into English.[3] She makes no use of any writing by Dalits or

---

3. See for example, Gayatri Chakravorty Spivak, 'Draupadi by Mahasweta Devi,' in *In Other Worlds: Essays in Cultural Politics*.

Adivasis themselves in her theorizing on subalternity. Limbale's book interrupts this process of writing the Dalit voice out of literary history and theory.

Literature sought, first, to erase the untouchable Other's existence and, then, to contain it. Literary history has followed this pattern. As I have suggested earlier, contemporary Indian literary history continues to be for the most part a history of upper caste Hindu writing. Its failure to recognize the writings of Dalits creates the impression that the treatment of Dalits and Adivasis in literature is due solely to the efforts of committed and progressive upper caste Hindu and other non-Dalit writers of goodwill. As far as literary history is concerned, Dalit writing is, to use Limbale's characterization, 'a nomad', much like the Dalits themselves, dwelling outside the boundary of the literary village.

Limbale, on the other hand, locates his tracing of the evolution of Marathi Dalit literature within the history of Marathi literature. He credits the contemporary progressive non-Dalit writers for opening the door for Dalit writing to appear. 'The rebellion of the new writers prised open the doors of Marathi literature, and created conditions favourable for the rise of Dalit literature,' he says. And, this, he suggests, was not a one-way street through which Dalit literature made its place in the stream of Marathi literature. This emergence of Dalit literature, he asserts, has been beneficial for Marathi literature as a whole. 'The horizon of Marathi literature and criticism has expanded and preferences have changed. Many new social strata have awakened and made literary contributions—because of Dalit literature.' Having entered the stream, Dalit literature has not merged into it, but has changed it.

The relationship of Dalit literature to the mainstream of Marathi literature is a conflicted one. According to the history that Limbale constructs, Marathi Dalit literature is related to upper caste Hindu literature in much the same way as the Dalit society is to the upper caste society: it is both a part of and yet apart from the mainstream. Through Dalit literature, the Dalit subaltern has now appeared in literature as a speaking subject, but this subaltern's speech is not interpellated by the dominant group's voice, language, tone, style or tradition.

Dalit literature is marked by a wholesale rejection of the tradition, the aesthetics, the language and the concerns of a Brahmanical literature that, even at its best, carried within it the signs of the caste-based social and cultural order. Instead, Dalit literature has established its own tradition with anti-caste or untouchable thinkers like Buddha, Kabir, Phule and Ambedkar as its signposts.

The speaking subject of this Dalit literature is the erstwhile untouchable Other of upper caste Hindu society, the occupant of the space outside the boundary of the village. The central concern of Dalit literature is how best to represent the 'authentic experience' of Dalits. Literary theory, whether classical Indian with its emphasis on the evocation of emotions and feelings (rasa) or contemporary western with its preoccupation with the unstable individual identity, is not found particularly useful, given the purpose as well as the focus of this literature. The authentic experience that Limbale refers to is that of a people, not just of an individual, and it is a seemingly unalterable experience, quite unlike that of any other group or community. The poor, the colonized or the ethno-racial minority, for example, can hope to alter their condition, not so the untouchable. Flowing from the condition of untouchability is a host of experiences that are unique and distinct. A number of questions immediately arise. What is this unique and distinct experience? What is involved in an authentic representation of this experience in literature? And what is the purpose of such representation?

Earlier in this commentary I have discussed the process by which Hindu society has constructed the Dalit subaltern as its Other. Dalitness is a condition for which it is very hard to find a parallel, though there may be certain similarities. Limbale compares the Dalit consciousness with that of a slave's. Other Dalit writers have drawn comparisons with African Americans and women.[4] Marxists, such as Sardesai, have argued for links being made between caste struggle and class struggle, and have been critical of Dalit leaders for their failure or refusal to do so. As if in answer to this criticism, Limbale defines Dalit in the broadest possible way to include all the dispossessed and oppressed of India:

> Harijans and neo-Buddhists are not the only Dalits. The term describes all the untouchable communities living outside the boundary of the village, as well as Adivasis, landless farm-labourers, the suffering masses, and nomadic and criminal tribes. In explaining the word, it will not do to refer only to the untouchable castes. People who are lagging behind economically will also need to be included.

I suggest that this is a political move on his part. He may well say here that untouchability is not the only reference point for defining the Dalit. However, the fact is that it is precisely the experiences that flow from a centuries-old hierarchical and hereditary system, unalterable because sanctioned by religion, with the concomitant notion of people as polluted and untouchable, which make the Dalit unique and distinct. All other experiences of exclusion, subjugation, dispossession and oppression, experiences that resemble those of other groups, result from this fundamental reality. Dalits may attain educational, economic, social and political success, but their unique Dalitness remains.

I do not use the term 'Dalitness' in an idealistic sense, nor in the sense of collapsing all the inner diversity and contradictions of Dalit life in some uniform and undifferentiated construct. The uniqueness of the Dalit experience, as Limbale suggests, rests in the fact that the core of Dalit materiality is

---

4. See, for example, Janardhan Waghmare, 'Black Literature and Dalit Literature'; and, Mohan Dass Naimishray, 'Stree Aarambh se Ant tak Dalit Hee Hai' ('Woman is a Dalit from Beginning to End'). Limbale himself has compared Dalit autobiographies with Black autobiographies for his doctoral thesis.

untouchability, which results in the naming of the Dalit as the unclean, impure Other.

It is the experience of this unique Dalitness that Dalit literature has been challenged to represent authentically. This has produced a literature that is at one level mimetic. A great deal of Dalit literature is in the genre of life writing. Not only has there been a preponderance of Dalit autobiographies, fictional writing, too, has used the biographical or autobiographical form to narrate the Dalit experience. These narratives seek to capture the authentic Dalit experience through a minute chronicling of the smallest detail of daily life in a language that, as Limbale terms it, is crude, impure and uncivil. It is as if, by capturing each detail, and reproducing it deliberately in a language that is the opposite of the language of upper caste literature, the Dalit writer will convey the essence of Dalitness. However, the mimetic representation that Dalit literature is concerned with is not that of the life of the individual but of the community. Here, again, it breaks sharply from the preoccupations of bourgeois literature. Thus, Sharan, the narrator-protagonist of Limbale's own work, *Akkarmashi*, though bearing many similarities with the author, is a composite character. The events and experiences that this character narrates are real in that they actually happened, though not necessarily to the narrator.[5] By making them part of Sharan's authentic experience, Limbale seems to suggest that each Dalit person's life partakes of the lives of all Dalits. Dalit poets use a similar strategy when they recuperate mythic figures such as Shambuka, Eklavya, Ravana and Shurpanaka from Hindu religious literature, and use them in portraying contemporary Dalit experience.[6] By thus communicating the continuity of Dalit experience through time and history, they make the point that the distinct and unique

5. See Vidyasagar Nautiyal, '*Akkarmashi*: Dalit Jwalamukhi' ('*Akkarmashi*: Dalit Volcano'); Sharankumar Limbale, '*Akkarmashi* ki Janmapatri' ('*Akkarmashi*'s Horoscope').

6. For example, Tryambak Sapkale's poems, 'Angulimal' and 'Eklavya,' in Anand and Zelliot, eds., *An Anthology of Dalit Literature*, 149–52.

Dalit experience has existed for a long time, and is not confined only to the quotidian reality of day-to-day existence in the present. This 'representationality', to use another of Limbale's term, makes the mimetic world of Dalit literature figurative.

The experience that Dalit literature represents is not always pleasant, nor constituted in terms of relations with the upper caste only. Dalit literature is unflinching in portraying the seamier side of Dalit life. Life outside the boundaries of the village, this literature seems to say, is marked by a sense of community, sharing, warmth and physicality. But it is also often wretched. There is in it ignorance, sexism, violence, internal rivalry and conflict, competition for survival, drunkenness and death. Authentic representation, then, involves an unromanticized and unpitying reflection in literature of the materiality of Dalit life in all its dimensions. Dalit (auto)biographical and fictional narratives and poetry neither hide nor romanticize anything. The people that inhabit these texts are not objects of pity. Their life is often miserable, humiliating, and filled with daily reminders of their impurity and pollutedness. These are signified by the wretchedness of their living conditions, their lawless or criminal pursuits, and their internalization of the oppressive ideas and habits of the Hindu caste society. But these are presented in Dalit literature without romanticization or glib defensiveness. At the same time, representation of Dalit life in this literature is not limited to an obsessive self-pitying narration of the misery and wretchedness of a people incapable of acting, as it is in much of the upper caste literature about Dalits. Dalits who people the texts of this literature may not be paragons of virtue, but they have life, they survive, struggle, and often succeed, even though their Dalitness – what Dangle calls 'differentness' (1994, viii) – never disappears. It is always-already there. It is this complex reality that constitutes the Dalits' authentic experience. This experience is spatial as well as temporal. Dalit literature is not ahistorical. The historicity of Dalit experience is conveyed, as I have suggested above, through the allusive nature of Dalit writing, its strategy of liberating certain figures of history and myth from the demonizing prison-hold of upper caste literature and using them to connect the present with the past.

Limbale characterizes Dalit literature as 'purposive', and describes its purpose variously as 'revolutionary', 'transformational' and 'liberatory'. One facet of Dalit literature's rejection of the Brahmanical literary tradition is that it does not adhere to classical Indian aesthetics, according to which the purpose of art and literature is to evoke different emotions and feelings, such as pity, love, fear and anger. Nor, as Limbale makes clear, does Dalit literature share either the devotional literature's other-worldly concerns, or the bourgeois literature's involvement with the desires, insecurities and alienation of the individual. And, finally, Dalit literature is neither a pleasure-giving literature of fine sentiments and refined gestures, nor a narcissistic wallowing in self-pity.

Being 'purposive', Dalit literature is, to use an old phrase, a literature of commitment. Contemporary Marathi Dalit literature emerged from a political movement – the Dalit Panthers – which many of these writers had been instrumental in founding. Dalit writers in other languages, though not involved in founding similar movements in their regions, also see themselves as part of a transformational movement. While some savarna writers may write out of a personal commitment to radical politics, or form groups due to a shared ideological or social agenda, no claim is made that all non-Dalit literature is revolutionary or transformational. The claim that Dalit literature is revolutionary and transformational is not based on the fact that all Dalit writers adhere to a radical ideology, such as socialism or Marxism. It rests on the view that, inasmuch as transforming the condition of the Dalit and challenging the caste system is a revolutionary cause, a literature that is entirely dedicated to this cause is, by definition, radical. The source of this radicalism is considered to be the thought and actions of Babasaheb Ambedkar.

Limbale argues that Dalit literature serves its radical function through its authentic representation of the Dalit reality. Through this representation, the untouchable Other finds voice to speak across the caste-line and thereby destroy the vaunted purity of the savarna space. The Dalit no longer remains invisible. This representation populates and contaminates the previously unpolluted sites of the savarna Hindu, and forces their occupants to come face-to-face with and recognize a reality that they brought into existence. This is a deconstructive enterprise. In the process of creating their authentic representations, Dalit writers expose and deconstruct those manufactured versions and processes of history and society that have been invoked through the centuries to legitimize the caste system.

This is one facet of the revolutionary project of Dalit literature. Its other, and perhaps more important facet, is the establishment of the full humanity of the Dalit. This literature asserts the Dalits' selfhood, history and agency. They are actors here, and not the ineffectual, helpless figures of the 'liberal-reformist' upper caste authors' creation, dependent on the goodwill and assistance of the dominant society for succour. In and through this literature, Dalits are no longer a people without history, much less the subalterns of society's history, its demonized Ravana or violated Angulimala, Eklavya or Shurpanaka. Here, they are the central figures of their own history, and from this history they derive the confidence and the right to assert their humanity. In this sense, perhaps the central purpose of Dalit literature is to enable the development of a new consciousness and identity among Dalits.

There is an interesting comparison to be made between Dalit literature's endeavour to construct a Dalit-centric identity and history, and Aimé Cesaire's concept of 'Negritude'.[7] Like Cesaire, Dalits have preferred an identity-based approach to politics, to Marxism's class-based approach. At the same time, Fanon's theorizing about racial identity development can be used profitably to examine the contemporary Dalit writers' location on the continuum of identity development (Fanon 1979).

---

7. See for example, Aimé Cesaire, *Discourse on Colonialism*; and Belinda Elizabeth Jack, *Negritude and Literary Criticism*, 57–79.

There is surely a difference between the coordinates of an older anti-caste writer-activist like Phule and those of a present-day Dalit writer-activist such as Limbale. Such a comparison might suggest that where the older generation of writer-activists was prepared to call on society's goodwill, and to collaborate with the ruling power of the day, the present generation has attained a level of confidence in its identity that it is ready and prepared to assert itself. The interest in the Black Nationalist movement of the 'African Americans, and the transformational agenda of today's Dalit literature, reflect that assertion.

Limbale argues that Dalit literature is 'unique' and 'distinct'. In this commentary, I have attempted to look at some of the key issues and considerations raised by him. The relationship of Dalits to the upper caste Hindu society is unparalleled. It is a relationship of domination–subordination, constituted by invoking the power of sacred texts. The literature that Dalit writers have created emerges from this relationship, and is an integral part of the political struggle to overturn it. In a profound sense, then, this literature engages with the Foucauldian Power/Knowledge paradigm.

Literary historians and theorists concerned with Indian literature written in the regional languages as well as English have generally failed so far to place and to deal with the implications of Dalit literature, largely because it does not fit into their theoretical frameworks. Extremely negative responses to the rereading of Premchand's canonical Hindi short story, 'Kafan', by Omprakash Valmiki, a Dalit writer and critic, as reported, for example, by Gautam (1996, 79), would suggest that the upper caste critics' unwillingness to seriously engage with Dalit writing and criticism is connected to their investment in Brahmanical canonical writing as universal. This view of Brahmanical literature and literary theory as canonical would have to be re-appraised and revised if Dalit writing were to be acknowledged as important. Methods and approaches of traditional Indian aesthetics are wholly inadequate to deal with the particularities of Dalit literature. Those associated with Subaltern Studies and Postcolonial Studies have not fared any better in evaluating or theorizing about Dalit literature, being caught up in the binary framework of the colonizer and the colonized.

In his controversial essay, 'Third-World Literature in the Era of Multinational Capital,' Frederic Jameson proposed another way of reading the so-called third world literature. He argued that all 'third-world texts ... are to be read as ... *national allegories*,' and, further, that '*the story of the private individual destiny is always an allegory of the embattled situation of the public third-world culture and society*' (1986, 69; author's emphasis). In a general sense, perhaps, Dalit literature accomplishes this, to the extent that the authentic experiences of the Dalit are a part and consequence of the conditions of India's public culture and society. But can it really be said that Dalit texts are 'national allegories', especially when Jameson defines the third world only in terms of its 'experience of colonialism and imperialism'? Yet, interestingly, even a radical critic like Aijaz Ahmad, who severely upbraided Jameson for taking this position and ignoring the fact that not all writers wrote back to the empire, being concerned, instead, about society's internal contradictions and complexities, has had nothing to say about the role and purpose of Dalit literature (Ahmad 1992, 95–122).

There is, curiously, a silence even among the most progressive, leftist critics to engage with this literature. One reason for this may be that very little of it is available in English. Most Dalit writers work in their first language, and are only now beginning to be translated. A bigger reason, I suggest, is that their work not only does not fit into neat binaries, in fact, it complicates them by exposing how a subjugated society such as that of pre-independence India could, simultaneously, be a subjugating society and how, in postcolonial India, that subjugation could continue. A further complicating fact is that Dalit writers and intellectuals do not fit clear ideological categories. Being Dalit-centric, these writers and intellectuals have reacted vehemently against any attempt that seemed designed to dilute the Dalit cause.

The exclusion of Dalit literature may help the non-Dalit to formulate neat theories and approaches, based on concepts of subalternity and postcoloniality, for example. It is clear that so long as this exclusion continues, these theories and approaches will remain incomplete—much like India itself.

2

About Dalit Literature

By Dalit literature, I mean writing about Dalits by Dalit writers with a Dalit consciousness. The form of Dalit literature is inherent in its Dalitness, and its purpose is obvious: to inform Dalit society of its slavery, and narrate its pain and suffering to upper caste Hindus.

Is it appropriate to expect pleasure or beauty, instead of inspiration for social transformation, from a literature that has been written primarily to raise awareness? Dalit writers believe that their literature should be analyzed from a sociological perspective focused on social values than on beauty. An exclusively aesthetic consideration of Dalit literature will disregard the Dalit writers' fundamental role, and hence is not acceptable to Dalit writers. Rejecting traditional aesthetics, they insist on the need for a new and distinct aesthetic for their literature—an aesthetic that is life-affirming and realistic. In other words, Dalit writers have demanded different yardsticks for the literary appraisal of their works. It is the firm conviction of Dalit writers and critics that if yardsticks change, the concept of aesthetics will change too.

Just as it is inappropriate to tell writers what and how they should write, similarly, it would be improper to dictate to critics the kind of criticism they should practise. It should also be remembered that the same work of art can be analyzed in different ways. This means that just as Dalit literature will be analyzed according to the role of Dalit writers, so too, criticism will be shaped by the role of the critic.

Upper caste critics have declared loudly that Dalit literature does not need a separate aesthetic, and that it should be critiqued on the basis of eternal values. But no one has engaged in an aesthetic analysis of Dalit literature after a serious reflection on the entirety of Dalit literature. In fact, even Dalit literary critics who have discussed the need for a separate aesthetic for Dalit literature have not performed exemplary criticism based on a careful and detailed reading of Dalit literature.

If an aesthetic consideration of Dalit literature is to be undertaken, it will be necessary to do so in the context of its uniqueness, inspiration, creation, role and features. This awareness has existed from the early days of Dalit literature. Instead of starting this discussion anew, we need to examine the perception and criticism of Dalit literature expressed until now. Otherwise, we will not be able to move forward.

Without such a comprehensive analysis encompassing the whole of Dalit literature, the criticism of Dalit literature, and Dalit literature itself, will not be able to move beyond the parameters within which they are circumscribed. In carrying out this analysis, it must be kept in mind that any aesthetic consideration of Dalit literature must be based on Ambedkar's thought, and that this literature's literary value is embedded in its social value.

Untruth: What is the place of 'satyam' in the lives of the Dalit, and the Adivasi? Is that truth about which such pride is expressed, and which is considered triumphant, really the truth?

Is it truth that the Brahman was born from Brahma's mouth and the Shudra from his feet? Is it truth that one is born a Shudra because of sins committed in a previous life?

Since there is no truth in any of this, satyam should really be asatyam.

Unholy: Hindu scriptures have deemed the touch, shadow and speech of the Dalit person as defiling. Food, water and people become impure from the touch of the untouchable. Not only human beings, even god becomes polluted. Separate settlements, riverbanks and cremation grounds have been arranged for untouchables.

For the nomadic and criminal tribes, there is neither village nor home. They have to wander constantly, and beg to live. What kind of shiva is this? These communities have to steal to survive. Human beings are deemed criminals by their birth. What sort of shiva is this?

Adivasis live the life of forest animals—what form of shiva is this?

Shudras serve the three upper varnas. They have no right to power, property, prestige and knowledge. Is this shiva?

Even today Dalits are tortured by being called Dalit. Injustice and ill treatment are inflicted on Dalit women.

This is the Hindu religious custom.

Unbeauty: Dalits should live outside the village; they should take inauspicious names; they should not accumulate property; they should possess only donkeys or dogs; and they should wear clothes meant to dress corpses. They should not learn Sanskrit or read the vedas, lest by doing so, they become aware of their oppression. They were forced to live an inauspicious, uncultured and untouchable life. But since they did not live mutely according to prescription, provision for serious punishment was made for any breach of the injunctions.

- Shambuka meditated, and was therefore killed.
- Eklavya acquired learning, but his thumb was cut off.
- Shivaji was called a Shudra when he laid claim to the throne.
- The dancer women of the Kolhati community adorn the beds of men. These rich upper caste Hindu men disrobe the women who perform nautanki. The women dance to please patrons in order to survive. How can they be expected to show spousal loyalty?

Satyam, shivam, sundaram—these are fabrications used to divide and exploit ordinary people. In fact, the aesthetic concept of 'satyam, shivam, sundaram' is the selfish mechanism of upper caste Hindu society. It is necessary to replace this conception of aesthetics with one that is material and social.

- Human beings are first and foremost human—this is satyam.
- The liberation of human beings is shivam.
- The humanity of human beings is sundaram.

Satyam, shivam, sundaram is a foolish aesthetic concept. There is no truth and beauty in the world comparable to that which is found in human beings. Therefore, it is essential to discuss the equality, liberty, justice and fraternity of human beings. In my opinion, that discussion will be the discussion of the aesthetics of Dalit literature.

3

Dalit Literature: Form and Purpose

3.1 INTRODUCTION

In the post-independence period, Marathi literature echoed with many literary streams. After India's independence, the spirit of nationalism gained strength in the society and in the hearts of the people. A fundamental transformation occurred in the lives of the people as a result of five-year plans, decentralization of power, public welfare schemes and spread of education. Common people began to understand the language of entitlements and rights due to the emergence of a democratic form of government. They felt that independence had set them free. Independence brought hope that all the issues facing the Indian people would be resolved. However, with time, the problems increased. Unemployment, poverty, growing population, communal conflicts, corruption in public life, the din of the Hindutva forces, and the ever-threatening spectre of famine led to a loss of popular faith in independence and saw the beginning of mass movements to seek redress for the various injustices.

Education and the idea of democracy reached many sections of the society, awakening the masses all over the country, as well as Dalits, Adivasis, and nomadic and criminal tribes living in and outside villages. The democratization of education enabled its spread among farmers, women and workers. The idea of the equal worth of all people was widely expressed, but social conditions did not change. There was revolutionary transformation in the lives of the nation, society and individuals due to the consciousness of such humanistic values as equality, liberty, fraternity and justice. Yet, at the same time, sentiments of pain and revolt were also kindled because of dissatisfaction with an inequitable system. The literatures of the post-independence period expressed these sentiments.

New writers emerged from various sections of the society. They presented in their writings, their own language, environment, condition and issues. Dalit literature attracted considerable discussion because its form and objective were different from those of the other post-independence literatures. Its presence was noted in India and abroad.

3.2 THE CREATION OF DALIT LITERATURE

The period from 'Mooknayak' to 'Mahanirvan', that is 1920 to 1956,[1] was influenced by the writings and political activities of Dr Babasaheb Ambedkar. He argued the case of untouchables from the boundaries of villages to Round Table conferences held by the British empire. He fought powerful forces, ranging from upper caste Hindu gatekeepers to god, for their rights. The entire Dalit society felt the impact of Babasaheb's work. How could Dalit writers be exceptions to this influence? They began to sing praises of his thought and action. The writings of several Dalit poets can be cited as examples. Through their writings, they raised consciousness in society about the need for struggle. The writing that took place during this phase propagated the message of revolution. This period of Babasaheb's work should be called the renaissance phase in the history of the Dalit movement. Bandhumadhav, Shankarrao Kharat and Annabhau Sathe were some of the prominent writers of this phase. The work of Dalit writer N R Shende was also being published during this period.

Babasaheb Ambedkar founded Siddhartha College in Mumbai, in 1946, and Milind College in Aurangabad, in 1947, for the

---

1. Translator's note: The period refers to Babasaheb Ambedkar's career spanning thirty-six years. It is the time between his work as the leader of the voiceless ('mooknayak') and his passing away soon after conversion to Buddhism ('mahanirvan').

higher education of Dalit boys. The first generation of Dalit students educated by these colleges was influenced by Babasaheb's thinking. The Dalit youth of this generation attempted to express their sentiments in writing. The annual publications of Milind College during that period bear testimony to this growing awareness.

In this early stage, savarna publishers and editors did not publish the writings of Dalit writers, not giving their work the slightest consideration. But Dalit writers persisted in writing and making every possible effort to be heard. Thus, the first conference of Dalit writers was held in the auditorium of Bengali High School, Dadar, on 2 March 1958. At this conference, a resolution was passed to the effect that the cultural importance of Dalit literature should be acknowledged and the literature given due recognition.

Babasaheb's religious conversion and nirvana had a momentous effect on the Dalit society. While the society gained a new cultural tradition from his conversion, his departure created a tremendous cultural vacuum. The Dalit leadership splintered into several groups, while injustices and atrocities against Dalits escalated. Questions of survival and physical repression intensified, giving rise to the feeling that the Dalit society had no defender.

Dalit youth acquired education in the post-independence period. They understood the importance of organization and struggle. The hope that their problems would be solved because of India's independence and the new constitution proved futile. On the one hand, there was a tremendous awakening in Dalit society due to knowledge, science and law; on the other hand, poverty and the caste system trapped them in a state of decrepitude. Spread of education, pressure of the Dalit movement, and struggle against conditions of existence caused Dalit youth to express their aversion for and anger against the established unequal social system in their writing. This writing, specifically, should be termed 'Dalit Literature'.

3.3 DALIT LITERATURE AND MARATHI LITERATURE

Ancient Marathi literature dwelt on the soul and the supreme soul. It could not progress beyond the binaries of desire and devotion. Ancient and modern Marathi literatures do not portray the actual life and struggle of the Marathi people; rather, they reflect the influence of the erotic and romantic aspects of Sanskrit and English literatures. In such a context, it would be surprising if the emergence of a literature that established the dignity of the untouchable person in powerful words did not become the subject of controversy. The emergence of Dalit literature caused a great disturbance in Marathi literature. Dalit writers began to write their literature unconcerned about any literary theories.

3.3.1 Sant Literature and Dalit Literature

The Marathi literature produced by the sants is said to be 'timeless literature'. Though the sants are revered by the Marathi people, the role of Dalit writers is different. The sants did not struggle against caste discrimination and for the deliverance of the untouchables. Moksha seemed more important to them, compared to social problems. They assuaged the women and the Shudras with mere sympathy. Though, in theory, the Dalit sants were equal at the doors of the gods, in practice, they were confined to the age-old lowest rung of the ladder. The helplessness of the Dalit sant writers signified by this situation, infuriates today's Dalit writers. Because of the caste system, Dalit writers have broken away from Hindu culture. It is therefore natural that they should feel a distance from the sants. The difference between the contemporary Dalit writers and the sants is not just a temporal difference, it is also the result of the cultural transformation that has taken place since the time of the sants.

Dalit writers reject the established tradition. This does not mean that they do not have a tradition. They claim the tradition of Buddha, Kabir, Phule and Ambedkar. Culture and tradition develop through the exchange of the new and the old, breaking the bounds of time. Just as this is true, so is it also true that a new rebel tradition is born out of the negation of the old. This rebel tradition has material knowledge of its own existence. It receives the endorsement of a large group, and acquires an independent existence. Eventually this new stream becomes an indivisible part of culture. The vedic tradition, rejecting the earlier non-vedic tradition, can be cited as an example of this process of tradition formation.

3.3.2 Modern Marathi Literature and Dalit Literature

The history of Marathi literature records the literary time-period from Keshavsut to Mardhekar – the pre-independance period – as 'modern'. Contemporary literature is considered to have begun after Mardhekar. In modern Marathi literature, Dalits have been portrayed from a middle-class perspective, which expresses sympathy for Dalits from a reformist-liberal standpoint. Because the middle-class, upper caste writers' world of experience is limited, there is no realistic representation of Dalits in their writing. In those writers who have portrayed Dalits, there is compassion, but there are no images of Dalits with self-pride.

Marathi literature began to assume a new face as a result of the terrible loss of life in the Second World War; the animal-like existence of human beings engendered by the machine age; the degradation of values; the influence of the ideas of Sartre, Camus, Kierkegaard and Freud; and the popular movements of the post-independence period. Compared to modern Marathi literature, the form and disposition of the new literature seemed different. However, this new literature's revolt was limited to changing literary values, its content persisted in revolving around middle-class life. Instead of delineating Dalits realistically, the new writers gave sensational descriptions of artificial sexuality, sensuality and crime. The revolutionary ideas of Dalit literature were not expressed in this writing. Even so, the monopoly of the high priests of Marathi literature received massive blows from this new literature, weakening their canonical authority. The rebellion of the new writers prised open the doors of Marathi literature, and created conditions favourable for the rise of Dalit literature.

The new writers' rebellion was not only literary in nature, it remained confined to Mumbai. The new writers wrote in an oppositional voice about the work of those who were published and promoted in literary magazines like *Satyakatha*. They demonstrated their dissatisfaction by burning copies of *Satyakatha*, which would not print their work. And they started publishing little magazines, which were not produced on a regular basis. The early writings of Raja Dhale and Namdeo Dhasal were published in these little magazines. Despite the friendly relationship between the new writers and these Dalit writers, differences can be seen in the form and purpose of their writings. Besides, the reasons for the rise of Dalit literature are different too.

3.3.3 Dalit Literature and Rural Literature

Rural literature was being written since 1925, but it came into its own only after independence. Eighty per cent of the population of Maharashtra lives in villages. With the spread of education, the sons of farmers began to make their presence felt, having learnt to read and write. Along with the dewdrops falling on the leaves of grass, they also saw the tears of the workers. The rural writers made the peasantry the centre of their literature.

Since much of Dalit literature is replete with portrayal of the villages, to the rural writers it appears to be part of rural literature. Village mohallas are settled along caste-lines. Outside the village are separate settlements, cremation grounds and wells for Dalits. For the nomadic and criminal tribes, there is neither a village nor a home; they are here today and elsewhere tomorrow. Begging or stealing is the only alternative available to them for filling their bellies. The Adivasi society leads an animal-like existence in the forests. Its contact with the village is limited to the weekly market. Despite the segregation, villagers torment Dalits, Adivasis, nomadic and criminal tribes. This is the real situation. Given this inequitable social reality, will it not be appropriate to identify all three communities with a single term—namely, Dalit?

Rural writers hold that if 'the experience of untouchability' or 'the stigma of caste system' is set aside, the lives of all the oppressed people are alike. However, to deny the visible presence of the caste system and say that all rural life is identical is to deny reality. It is not possible to close one's eyes to the experience of the untouchable, because it is the experience of thousands of people over thousands of years. Dalit literature is born from the womb of this untouchability. This is its uniqueness.

Only Dalit writers have narrated the pain of Dalits—this is as true as the fact that rural writers have not depicted the life of Dalits. This defines the limit of the rural writers' experience. It is as incongruous to expect those who write for entertainment to write Dalit literature, as it is for Dalit writers to write for entertainment. Writers write according to their natural preference. To say that they should write in a particular way is to impose the burden of one's expectation on them. Every reader could have a different expectation, which makes it impossible for writers to write according to others' expectations. The proper course is to evaluate what has been written in its specific, unique context.

Dalits have voiced their dissatisfaction against the unequal Hindu caste system. Ambedkar's thoughts are the source of this dissatisfaction. Rural literature does not talk about the caste system. The inspiration for the two literatures is also different. For these reasons, Dalit literature is distinct from rural literature. There is as much dissimilarity between these, as there is between the savarna society living in the village and the untouchable society living outside the boundary of the village.

There has not been a realistic delineation of Dalits in ancient, modern and contemporary Marathi literatures. In order to provide a realistic portrait of Dalits, Dalit writers will have to write. And Dalit writers have written, inspired by the purpose of depicting in literature the authentic experiences of Dalit life.

3.4 WHO IS DALIT?

To start with, there will have to be a definite explanation of the word 'Dalit' in Dalit literature. Harijans and neo-Buddhists are not the only Dalits, the term describes all the untouchable communities living outside the boundary of the village, as well as Adivasis, landless farm-labourers, workers, the suffering masses, and nomadic and criminal tribes. In explaining the word, it will not do to refer only to the untouchable castes. People who are lagging behind economically will also need to be included.

3.5 WHAT IS DALIT LITERATURE?

Dalit literature is precisely that literature which artistically portrays the sorrows, tribulations, slavery, degradation, ridicule and poverty endured by Dalits. This literature is but a lofty image of grief.

Every human being must find liberty, honour, security, and freedom from intimidation by the powerful elements of society. These values are now being articulated in a particular kind of literature—its name being Dalit literature. Recognizing the centrality of the human being, this literature is thoroughly saturated with humanity's joys and sorrows. It regards human beings as supreme, and leads them towards total revolution.

3.5.1 Suffering in Dalit Literature

The Hindu religious order has considered the Dalits' shadow, touch and speech to be impure. It has regarded them untouchable and guilty from birth. Dalits should not accumulate property or wear gold ornaments, they should live outside the village and own only donkeys and dogs. Furthermore, they should partake of food only in clay utensils, use only shrouds for clothing, and take inauspicious and crude names. Hindu scriptures are replete with numerous such commands.

For thousands of years, Dalits have been kept deprived of power, property and position. It was propounded that 'god created this hierarchy', so that Dalits may not rebel against this social order. Thousands of generations of Dalits have continued to endure this injustice.

Dalit society came to understand its slavery following the thoughts of Babasaheb Ambedkar. This mute society found its hero in Babasaheb, and its anguish voice through him. This anguish of Dalits is the progenitor of Dalit literature. It is not the pain of any one person, nor is it of just one day—it is the anguish of many thousands of people, experienced over thousands of years. Therefore, it is expressed collectively. The anguish of Dalit literature is not that of an individual but of the entire outcast society. This is the reason why it has assumed a social character.

3.5.2 Rejection and Revolt in Dalit Literature

'Rejection' and 'revolt' in Dalit literature have been birthed from the womb of Dalits' pain. They are directed against an inhuman system that was imposed on them. Just as the anguish expressed in Dalit literature is in the nature of a collective social voice, similarly, the rejection and revolt are social and collective.

This rejection is aimed at the unequal order which has exploited Dalits. Its form is double-edged—rejecting the unequal order, and demanding equality, liberty, fraternity and justice. To use a legal concept, the rejection in Dalit literature constitutes a 'just remedy'.

Revolt is the stage that follows anguish and rejection. 'I am human, I must receive all the rights of a human being'—such is the consciousness that gives birth to this revolt. Born from unrestrained anguish, this explosive rejection and piercing revolt is like a flood, with its aggressive character and an insolent, rebellious attitude.

3.5.3 Experience in Dalit Literature

The experiences articulated in Dalit literature have not yet been expressed in any other literature. They are the experiences of a particular community. Experiences conveyed in Dalit literature have several characteristics. They constitute an engagement in self-search to achieve self-respect; and the rejection of traditions and a religion that are opposed to such self-respect. They mark a rebellion against overbearing religion and tradition, as well as hypocrisy masquerading under seductive names such as freedom or democracy. They express the pain of human beings who are not treated as human. They demonstrate respect for the Buddhist value of treating humans as human. And they nurture the feeling of unending gratitude towards Dr Babasaheb Ambedkar and Mahatma Phule.

Dalit writers assert that their literature conveys the life that they have lived, experienced and seen. Since the experience contained in Dalit literature is articulated out of a desire for freedom, its character is collective rather than individual. It is this experience that has inspired Dalit writers to write. The connection of experience with the lives of Dalits cannot be ignored. Experience, here, is the product prepared from a chemical process, with pain and revolt as the ingredients. Dalit consciousness plays a prominent role in this.

3.5.4 Dalit Consciousness

The Dalit consciousness in Dalit literature is the revolutionary mentality connected with struggle. It is a belief in rebellion against the caste system, recognizing the human being as its focus. Ambedkarite thought is the inspiration for this consciousness. Dalit consciousness makes slaves conscious of their slavery. Dalit consciousness is an important seed for Dalit literature, it is separate and distinct from the consciousness of other writers. Dalit literature is demarcated as unique because of this consciousness.

3.5.5 Commitment in Dalit Literature

Dalit writers make their personal experiences the basis of their writing. Always prominent in their writing is the idea that certain notions have to be revolted against, some values have to be rejected, and some areas of life have to be strengthened and built upon. Because Dalit writers write from a predetermined certitude, their writing is purposive.

Dalit writers write out of social responsibility. Their writing expresses the emotion and commitment of an activist. That society may change and understand its problems—their writing articulates this impatience with intensity. Dalit writers are activist-artists who write while engaged in movements. They regard their literature to be a movement. Their commitment is to the Dalit and the exploited classes.

But Dalit writers' voicings can be negatively influenced by their commitment. It is necessary for them to know the boundary between the activist and the artist. The writer's creation is a part of social life. Transformational writers cannot shirk social responsibility. Even so, it is important for them to ensure that this responsibility does not have a harmful effect on their creation.

3.5.6 The Language of Dalit Literature

The view of life conveyed in Dalit literature is different from the world of experience expressed hitherto. A new world, a new society and a new human being have been revealed in literature, for the first time. The reality of Dalit literature is distinct, and so is the language of this reality. It is the uncouth-impolite language of Dalits. It is the spoken language of Dalits. This language does not recognize cultivated gestures and grammar. It is said that language changes after every twenty miles, but this arithmetic turns out to be wrong with respect to Dalits. In the same village, differences are evident between the language of the village and the language of the untouchable quarters.

For their writing, Dalit writers have used the language of the quarters rather than the standard language. Standard language has a class. Dalit writers have rejected the class of this standard language. Cultured people in society consider standard language to be the proper language for writing. Dalit writers have rejected this validation of standard language by the cultured classes, because it is arrogant. To Dalit writers, the language of the basti seems more familiar than standard language. In fact, standard language does not include all the words of Dalit dialects. Besides, the ability to voice one's experience in one's mother tongue gives greater sharpness to the expression.

Dalit writers have reacted bitterly to Hindu religious literature. Despite the fact that epics are literature, Dalit society is not accurately portrayed in them. The epics depict people from the 'low' castes as using Prakrit. The fact is that Shudras were prohibited from learning Sanskrit, since it was regarded as the language of the gods. (Because of this reason, Babasaheb was not able to study Sanskrit; instead, he had to study Farsi.) 'Rama, the killer of Shambuka, cannot be our ideal. *Gita* and *Mahabharata*, which support the caste system, cannot be honoured by us': this is the perspective of Dalit writers.

Dalit writers have used those images and symbols in their literature that are appropriate for relating experiences. Use of distinct images and symbols is seen especially in Dalit poetry. However, Dalit writers cannot forget that Hindu religious literature has nourished the unequal caste system. Therefore, they have decided not to use religious symbols in their writing. Dalit critics have encouraged Dalit writers to construct new myths instead of using the existing symbols and metaphors of Hindu sacred literature. When the Dalit writers did employ religious symbols, it was to deconstruct them, infusing them with new meaning and purpose.

3.6   CHARGES AGAINST DALIT LITERATURE

Because of the form, purpose and role of Dalit literature, many accusations have been made against it. It has been charged that Dalit literature is propagandist, univocal and negative; that it does not represent the individual person; and, that excessive resentment is heard in Dalit literature.

3.6.1   Is Dalit literature Propagandist?

Dalit literature has been criticized as being propagandist. It has been alleged that this literature lacks artistic finesse, and that

Dalit writers affect a 'pose' when they write. It has been charged further, that their writing expresses the frenzy of a movement, and does not possess neutrality and objectivity.

If Dalit literature appears to be propagandist, it is because it presents the Dalit writers' anguish and their questions. This literature has made a declaration for human values, and hence is not neutral. Dalit writers cannot sever their relationship with their pain. The questions they pose in their work are their own, and those of their society—they cannot be neutral. To the critics, their reaction may seem like a pose. However, it cannot be said that the entire corpus of Dalit literature is propagandist. Since Dalit writers see their writing as a means of human liberation, expressing emotion is integral to the literature they produce. Intense lived and felt experiences cannot be called propagandist.

3.6.2 Is Dalit Literature Univocal?

Dalit literature is also frequently accused of being mired in univocality, monotony and stasis. The source of this univocality is the expression of an ideological view common to all Dalit literature. Because of this common ideological function, the character of this literature is univocal. Besides, the experiences narrated in Dalit literature are very similar. Untouchables' experiences of untouchability are identical. The name of the village may well be different, but the nature of tyranny against Dalits is the same. Social boycott, separate bastis, wells and cremation grounds; inability to find rental accommodation; the necessity to conceal caste; denial of admission to public places; injustices done to Dalit women; dragging and cutting of dead animals; and the barber refusing to cut hair—these experiences are alike for all Dalits. For example, there are many similarities between the episodes about skinning of animals in *Aathwaninche Pakshi* and *Akkarmashi*.

Because of the commonalities in Dalit writers' thoughts, experiences and emotions, Dalit literature appears to be univocal. Though not as evident in prose, the univocality is felt especially in Dalit poetry.

3.6.3 Is there No Individual in Dalit Literature?

A unique feature of Dalit literature is its collective aspect. The experience described in Dalit literature is social, hence it is articulated as collective in character. Therefore, even when the experience expressed in Dalit literature is that of an individual, it appears to be that of a group. For this reason, it is alleged that there is no individual in Dalit literature.

3.6.4 Is Dalit Literature Resentful?

Dalit literature has also been accused of being resentful, and it has been said that this resentment is akin to breast-beating. In fact, to the Dalit writer, this resentment does not feel like resentment; it seems like the suppressed irritation of many years. This resentment is the expression of anguish, rage and rebellion. The anger expressed in Dalit literature is its natural disposition.

Societally caused anguish has bred resentment among Dalits. This anguish remained silenced until it found a voice in the person of Babasaheb Ambedkar. Since then the pain has gushed forth like a burst dam. It is inappropriate to expect this pain to be restrained and artistic. It had remained suppressed for thousands of years. Now, the expectation of liberation has given it an explosive form.

3.6.5 Why an Independent Existence for Dalit Literature?

Initially, absolutely no notice was taken of Dalit literature. Emerging Dalit writers established their own literary organizations and brought out their own magazines. By organizing Dalit literature conferences, identity festivals and theatre conferences, they asserted an independent space for Dalit literature. This independent and separate literary stream of Dalit writers was much discussed, causing savarna writers to question the need for a 'separate hearth'.

Dalit writers argued that Dalit literature was distinct, and needed an independent space for itself, since the reality of Indian society and mentality had not changed. Given the persistence of the traditional village system with untouchable settlements outside the boundaries, conventional ideas, and dishonesty in allocation of positions reserved for historically excluded communities, how is it possible that Dalit literature will not seek autonomy?

The singular identity of Dalit literature is revealed through its rebellious, collective character; the Dalit writers' distinct experience, their use of folk language, their commitment to human liberation; and the influence of Ambedkar's thought.

3.7 CONTRIBUTION OF DALIT LITERATURE TO INDIAN LITERATURE

Dalit literature is a new and distinct stream of Indian literature. It has contributed to Indian literature fresh experiences, a new sensitivity and vocabulary, a different protagonist, an alternate vision, and a new chemistry of suffering and revolt. Indian literary criticism has also been stimulated to introspect, and fundamental questions have been raised in the minds of readers and critics.

Because of Dalit literature the process of social convergence began, and the winds of change became brisk. Many Dalits started writing, and writers emerged from different strata of society. The horizon of Indian literary criticism expanded and readers' tastes changed. The significance of Dalit literature in the larger canvas of Indian literature is clear.

3.8 THE FUTURE OF DALIT LITERATURE

The questions beginning to emerge now are: How long will Dalit literature remain distinct and new? What is the future of this literature? Dalit writers believe that so long as this unequal order remains, Dalit literature will also exist.

An unfair system that has existed for thousands of years will not be destroyed overnight. Several more years will be needed for its complete destruction. Till then the literary revolt of the displaced against the established order will continue.

3.9 CONCLUSION

Due to Babasaheb Ambedkar, Dalit society began to organize and struggle. Writers close to Babasaheb were influenced by his work. They wrote with the aim of disseminating his thoughts and actions.

The creativity of Dalit literature has to be considered in the context of Babasaheb Ambedkar's agitations, his thought, his religious conversion; the social, economic and political events of the post-independence period; and the vacuum left in Dalit society on Babasaheb's death. Dalit writers have been inspired to write because of the popularization of education, the spread of democracy, science and law, as well as the organizing and the struggles of Dalit youth.

Historically, Dalits were not portrayed truthfully or with fairness, from the time of Hindu religious literature to contemporary Marathi literature. Therefore Dalit writers reject this alienating literary tradition and write with the objective of explaining to people their own pain, problems and questions. Because of their commitment, and the inspiration of Ambedkar's thought, Dalit literature has acquired the form of a movement.

In order to stabilize the stream of Dalit literature within the larger flow of Marathi literature, organized discussions, conferences and seminars have taken place, and little magazines and their special issues have been published. There has been considerable writing from the beginning in terms of Dalits' pain, rejection, revolt, experience, language and commitment, as well as the aspersions cast against Dalit literature. Dalit writers and critics have attempted to explain every defining word. They have answered the questions raised in relation to Dalit literature: Who should be called Dalit? What is the meaning of Dalit literature? Should Dalit literature be recognized as distinct from other literatures?

There have been many proponents and opponents of Dalit literature because of the new experiences, the distinct language, the revolutionary ideology, the aggressive character, the refusal of inequality, and the declaration of the triumph of human values ingrained in it. There have been discussions both in favour of and against it, and Dalit literature has burgeoned. The horizon of Marathi literature and criticism has expanded and preferences have changed. Many new social strata have awakened and made literary contributions because of Dalit literature.

4

Dalit Literature and Ambedkarism

4.1 INTRODUCTION

Babasaheb Ambedkar converted to Buddhism on 14 October 1956. Inspired by his action, a large number of Dalits gave up Hinduism,[1] and rejected its gods and goddesses. They abandoned the mean tasks that the upper caste Hindus forced them to perform, and harassed them if they refused. Consequently, a new kind of discord emerged between the savarnas and the Dalits, who opted for a different identity as a result of this upheaval. A new consciousness was awakened in Dalit society: 'We have become Buddhists, therefore, we will no longer perform the mean tasks imposed on us by the Hindu religion.'

The Dalit literature movement sunk its roots during this period of cultural transition. Therefore, neo-Buddhist scholars expected that this new literary movement would be evaluated in the context of Buddhist thought. Attempts were made to analyze Dalit literature using Buddhist and Ambedkarite perspectives.

4.2 DALIT LITERATURE AND BUDDHISM

The mass conversion to Buddhism brought about a revolutionary change in the consciousness of Dalit society. The historical event marked the beginning of a new liberation struggle. Dalits

---

1. Translator's note: Barbara Joshi says: 'In 1956, Ambedkar joined 500,000 of his followers in a Buddhist conversion ceremony.' See Joshi, ed., *Untouchable! Voices of the Dalit Liberation Movement*, 28.

found a new cultural dimension in Buddhism, and it had an energizing impact on the development of Dalit literature.

There is no place for a caste system in Buddhism, which supports egalitarianism and rejects inequality. Babasaheb embraced Buddhism because Buddha rejected casteism and admitted everyone into his religion.

After Babasaheb's death, the Dalit society tried to assimilate and disseminate the tenets of Buddhism through different actions and practices. These included marrying according to the Buddhist custom, naming children and homes in accordance with Buddhism, celebrating Buddha Jayanti, establishing new vihars, following the Panchasheel and Trisharan, respecting Buddhist monks, and working as propagators of Buddhism. This process also included the privileging of Buddhist literature.

4.2.1 Founding of Maharashtra Boudha Sahitya Parishad

Dalit literature was being published even before Babasaheb Ambedkar's conversion. The first mass conversion of Dalits took place on 14 October 1956, and the first literary conference of Dalit writers was held on 2 March 1958. Significantly, it was called a conference on Dalit rather than Buddhist literature. In 1949, Dalit writers had established an organization, Dalit Sevak Sahitya Sangha, on the insistence of Appasaheb Ranapise. In 1950, the name of the organization was changed to Dalit Sahitya Sangha in accordance with Yadav Piraji Tippal's proposal of 2 October 1950. On 11 March 1960, the name of the organization was again altered to Maharashtra Boudha Sahitya Parishad.

Discussions of Dalit literature began during this period from 2 March 1958 to 11 March 1960. This was also the time when the 'progressive literature' of Communist writers and the 'little magazine' literature of the new writers were being published. Dalit writers sided with these movements. Concerned that Dalit writers should not turn away from the Buddhist literary tradition, the group of Dalit writers that had converted to

Buddhism began to promote Buddhist literature.[2] They took an adversarial position towards progressive literature on the ground that the inspiration of Communism was life-destroying.

Having accepted Buddhism, it was necessary to create Buddhist literature. To them the word 'Dalit' was anathema, and must be rejected. They held that the term Dalit had no culture. In contrast, for the Dalit writers, the term was emblematic of an egalitarian revolution. In Marathi literature, Dalit literature stood for universal freedom. The word Dalit did not denote caste; rather, it referred to those who were yesterday's exploited and were now fighting back. Thus, while the neo-Buddhist writers have ridiculed the word Dalit, Dalit writers have embraced it. Today, the term Dalit has acquired a new dimension; it does not seem appropriate for neo-Buddhist writers to criticize it.

4.2.2 Support for Buddhist Literature

In Dalit society, conversion led to increased reverence for and curiosity about Buddhism, and a desire to propagate it. Neo-Buddhist writers took the position that Dalit writers should create Buddhist literature because of the intellectual and inspirational power of Buddhist philosophy.

Buddhist literature was first produced in Pali and Sanskrit, and with the spread of Buddhism, in Burmese, Chinese, Tibetan and Sinhala languages. Neo-Buddhist critics have suggested that Dalit writers should study Buddhist literature in all these languages. Their proposal seems like an edict. First, we will have to consider how many Dalit writers are familiar with these languages. Second, we will have to keep in mind that the original Buddhist literature in these languages is of a religious nature, whereas the literature of Dalit writers is social in nature. And, there is a great difference between the times of Lord Buddha and of the Dalit writers. Today, though the ancient sant literature is still being read, it is no longer being created. Just so, preserving

---

2. Translator's note: Limbale uses the term 'neo-Buddhist writers' to refer to those Dalit writers who converted to Buddhism.

Buddhist literature does not amount to creating Buddhist literature. The form and content of contemporary Buddhist literature will differ from that of ancient Buddhist literature.

Neo-Buddhist writers can use one of two approaches. They can rebel against the established social order of savarna society which is responsible for leading us into the present situation. Or, they can take the position, 'My life is separate from that of others.' Possibly, better quality literature can be produced by utilizing the second approach, as it attaches greater importance to distinctive experience than to revolt. The approach also insists that this distinct experience is worth narrating. But the neo-Buddhist thinkers have not clarified what is worth narrating.

Although a large section of the Dalit society has converted to Buddhism, some time must pass before it can become completely Buddhist. And it will take just as long to create Buddhist literature. In these circumstances, expecting Buddhist literature from Dalit writers is, if not inappropriate, certainly undesirable. This is the truth.

4.2.3 The Nature of Buddhist Criticism

Thinkers who support Buddhist literature have criticized Dalit literature. For example, Vijay Sonwane says: 'Our ancestors dragged animal carcasses, fed on leavings, begged—did all sorts of things. Is any compassion ever aroused in savarna society because of these? Why then should our untouchability be repeatedly put on display at the crossroads? Why should we humiliate our own society?' (Sonwane 1979, 27). It is necessary to answer such questions.

Sonwane has questioned whether any compassion was ever aroused in savarna society about Dalit society. Reading Dalit literature may or may not arouse feelings in savarna society; this literature is written with the primary objective of making Dalit society aware of its slavery. It is erroneous to think that Dalit writers should not create Dalit literature because savarna society does not respond to it. It is out of place for Sonwane to ask, 'Why should we repeatedly put our untouchability on display at the crossroads?' The fact is that public display of the injustices and ill treatment inflicted on us is indeed the purpose of Dalit literature. It is incongruous to believe that the injustices and excesses done to one's society should not be publicly exposed for fear that this may humiliate one's community.

Promiscuity and immorality have not been the exclusive attributes of Dalits. Promiscuity seems to prevail in every society. D K Kharpade has posed the question: 'Why should the Dalit writer, born out of promiscuity, write an autobiography?' (Kharpade 1990). Kharpade criticizes this kind of writing because, to him, it appears to humiliate Dalit society. But the viewpoint of Dalit critics is the opposite of Kharpade's. Dalit writers have narrated their experiences boldly, unconcerned about shame or fear. Dalit critics have supported the work of Dalit writers, whereas neo-Buddhists have ridiculed Dalit literature. The criticism of neo-Buddhist thinkers is the product of a middle-class mentality. It is symbolic of their narrow perspective.

Dalit writers regard promiscuity as rape, because it is the result of injustices committed by affluent, savarna males towards penniless, untouchable women. The neo-Buddhist thinkers disagree. Mohan Raosaheb has gone so far in his criticism as to say that savarna critics have incited those Dalit writers who disgrace Dalit society, and then glorified their writing (Raosaheb 1990). He has made several observations about savarna criticism. According to him, the savarna critics have suppressed or ignored the literature of revolutionary ideas. They have incited writers with a revolutionary heritage to produce a literature that parades the sorrow of their own caste in public, instead of engaging in total social revolution. And, they have made a special effort to engender among Dalit writers respect for Brahmanical literature and its practitioners.

Mohan Raosaheb's conclusions are one-sided. It does not appear that Dalit literature has been suppressed by savarna society, nor have savarnas issued any strict injunction that Dalit writers must write only about their society's sorrow. It is evident that Brahmanical literature and Brahmanical writers have always assumed an oppositional stance vis-à-vis Dalit writers. Given this context, it can only be said that Raosaheb's conclusions are not based on ground reality. Some savarna writers have certainly asked Dalit writers to write about the sorrows of their caste, and have published those texts, but we cannot conclude from this that they have suppressed revolutionary ideas. Raosaheb's criticism does not seem apposite.

4.2.4 Limitations of Buddhist Criticism

Neo-Buddhist writers wrote extensively in the early phase of Dalit literature. Subsequently, Dalit writers began to emerge from different Dalit castes as well as Adivasi sub-castes and nomadic and criminal tribes, besides the neo-Buddhist writers. This is the reason why Vasant Moon has asked: 'Not all untouchables are Buddhist, not all Dalit writers are Buddhist. Will it be said that these are not our people?' (Moon 1982). It would be desirable to adopt a comprehensive position on whether Buddhist literature will only be the literature of the neo-Buddhists, and whether or not the literature of Dalit and Advasi writers from different castes and sub-castes, and writers from the nomadic and criminal tribes can be included in it.

Neo-Buddhist literary critics have not explained how Buddha's karmasiddhant, avtarvad, rebirth and nirvana can be linked to Dalit literature. In the Buddhist period, one's caste was destroyed when one entered Buddha's sangha. But, even after Dalits accepted Buddhism, the injustices and the ill treatment meted out to them due to communal feelings did not stop. The exploitation of Dalits did not end through the ashtang marg or sikkhapad enunciated by Buddha. The misery that Buddha saw was born out of human desire, but the source of the Dalits's sorrow is different—it is the product of Hinduism's caste system. Neo-Buddhist thinkers have not reflected seriously on this difference.

4.3 THE CREATIVE INSPIRATION FOR DALIT LITERATURE

The period dating from the Southborough Commission of 27 January 1919, to 6 December 1956, constitutes the backbone of Dalit literature. This period was influenced by the work and accomplishments of Babasaheb Ambedkar. A number of historic occurrences influenced the Dalit movement, including the few reformist movements against an unequal social system, thousands of years old; the rapidly growing national movement of the Congress; the political importance gained by minorities during foreign rule; the piecemeal concessions extracted from the British; the visits of British commissions to India; the Round Table conferences; elections; the Second World War; Indian independence; partition; the religious conversion of Dalits; and Babasaheb Ambedkar's establishment as the leader of the Dalits.

The story of Babasaheb's life, his work, ideas and message awakened the Dalit society, the Dalit movement and the Dalit writers. Ambedkarite ideology is the true inspiration for Dalit literature. Dalit society found self-respect through Babasaheb's ideas and agitations. We would not *be*, if there had been no Babasaheb. The practice of uttering *Jai Bhim* when greeting each other in Dalit society symbolizes this inspirational role.

4.4 AMBEDKARISM

Ambedkarism is a modern idea for ending the caste system. Babasaheb fought against this iniquitous system in Hinduism that fostered inequality. Following are the manifestations of the caste system:

1. Heredity: The child belongs to the same caste as the parents.

2. Marriage restrictions: Marriage outside one's own caste is prohibited.

3. Profession: Taking up the work of another caste while giving up one's paternally inherited profession is banned.

| 4. Dietary rules: | Distinction is made not only between vegetarian and meat-based diets, but even touching the food and water of people seen as inferior, and from a different religion, is prohibited. |
| 5. Hierarchy: | Some castes are regarded as upper and others lower. |

The caste system has exploited the Dalits and imposed painful restrictions on them. Dalit society was robbed due to its weakness, poverty and ignorance—causing Babasaheb to talk about building self-respect. He said that Dalits must gain the strength to take the reins of power and enact laws. These were new and revolutionary ideas for Dalits, who had been living a life marked by helplessness and lack of options, subject to the slavery that was imposed on them.

Babasaheb's ideas about social justice are evident in his defence of the untouchables before the Southborough Commission, the Simon Commission, and the Round Table conferences; his publications, such as *Mook Nayak, Bahishkrit Bharat, Janata* and *Samata*; his efforts with the Bahishkrit Hitkarini Sabha, Majoor Paksha, Scheduled Caste Federation and the Republican Party of India; his entry into the Kala Ram temple; his leadership role in the Chavdar Lake agitation of the Mahars, and the burning of *Manusmriti*; his participation in meetings, conferences and gatherings; his founding of Siddhartha College and Milind College; his work in formulating the Indian Constitution; and his acceptance of Buddhism.

In a speech broadcast by All India Radio on 3 October 1954, in the series 'My Personal Philosophy', Babasaheb said:

Positively, my social philosophy may be said to be enshrined in three words: liberty, equality and fraternity. Let no one however say that I have borrowed my philosophy from the French Revolution. I have not. My philosophy has roots in religion and not in political science. (Keer 1987, 459)

As his biographer, Dhananjay Keer, says:

> In his philosophy, law had a place only as a safeguard against the breaches of liberty and equality; but he did not believe that law can be a guarantee for breaches of liberty or equality. He gave the highest place to fraternity as the only real safeguard against the denial of liberty or equality or fraternity —which was another name for brotherhood or humanity, which was again another name for religion. (Keer 1987, 459)

Babasaheb accorded an extremely important place to humanity in his thought system. Indeed, humanism is synonymous with Ambedkarism, because Ambedkarite thought is creative thought about fighting against the devaluation of human beings.

4.5 AMBEDKARITE LITERARY THOUGHT

Babasaheb has a definite life-affirming and realistic position on literature. His literary perspective becomes clear from his comment on the vedas: 'I have read the *Rigveda* and the *Atharvaveda* many times. But what is there in them about societal and human progress and ethical conduct that is persuasive, this I cannot understand' (Ambedkar 1944). Babasaheb believed that literature should not only promote social and human progress, but also foster values. He says: '*Manusmriti* is not acceptable to us, given its endorsement of inequality. Why should we not burn such a text?' (Ambedkar 1928a). In 1938, more than ten years after the burning of *Manusmriti*,[3] he explained in an interview with T V Parvate:

---

3. Translator's note: On 25 December 1927 in Mahad, Maharashtra, Babasaheb led an agitation to assert the equal rights of Dalits to draw water from the city's Chavdar Lake. The day-long agitation culminated in the evening, in a mass meeting of Dalits in which several resolutions were passed demanding equal rights. The climax of the meeting was the burning of the *Manusmriti* (*The Laws of Manu*) in a bonfire. Ambedkar undertook the symbolic act of burning this sacred text because its author, the ancient sage Manu, is credited with codifying the laws of untouchability and pollution. For a detailed account of this dramatic event, see Keer, *Dr. Ambedkar: Life and Mission.*

It is not that all the parts of *Manusmriti* are condemnable, that it does not contain good principles and that Manu himself was not a sociologist and was a mere fool. We made a bonfire of it because we view it as a symbol of injustice under which we have been crushed across centuries. Because of its teachings we have been ground down under despicable poverty. (Keer 1987, 106).

A literature that supports inequality is not only unacceptable to him, in his view there must be a mass movement against such literature. He did not stop with saying that *Manusmriti* was unacceptable to him. He, in fact, publicly burned it. According to him, every text must be accountable to society and to humanity. He took the position that literature must enhance equality and destroy inequality. For Babasaheb, sant literature failed this test because it was of no use in the destruction of the Hindu varna system.

Babasaheb Ambedkar posed the question: 'Why could a Voltaire not be born in our country?' (Ambedkar 1927a). Voltaire's literature caused a revolution. An oppressive state was overturned and common people were released from subjugation. Today, there is need for a talent like Voltaire's. But Babasaheb did not think that an Indian Voltaire could emerge from the ranks of Brahman scholars, for the cost would be too high.

[Today] all scholarship is confined to the Brahmins. But unfortunately no Brahmin scholar has so far come forward to play the part of a Voltaire who had the intellectual honesty to rise against the doctrines of the Catholic Church in which he was brought up; nor is one likely to appear on the scene in the future ... Why have the Brahmins not produced a Voltaire?... It must be recognized that the selfish interest of a person or of the class to which he belongs always acts as an internal limitation which regulates the direction of his intellect ... As is natural, every Brahmin is interested in the maintenance of Brahmanic superiority be he orthodox or unorthodox, be he a priest or a *grahastha*, be he a scholar or not. How can the Brahmins afford to be Voltaires? A Voltaire among the Brahmins would be a positive danger to the maintenance of a civilization which is contrived to maintain Brahamanic supremacy. (Ambedkar 1990, 240)

Writers emerging from amongst Dalit, exploited and deprived societies must accept this call for a Voltaire. But in order to be a Voltaire, one must stand up to religion and state, for they sanction exploitation. Hindu writers have defended *Manusmriti*, being agents of the established order. Babasaheb asserted that writers should take inspiration from the greatness of common people:

> Through your literary creations cleanse the stated values of life and culture. Don't have a limited objective. Transform the light of your pen so that the darkness of villages is removed. Do not forget that in our country the world of the Dalits and the ignored classes is extremely large. Get to know intimately their pain and sorrow, and try through your literature to bring progress in their lives. True humanity resides there. (Ambedkar 1976, 8)

Babasaheb's literary thought is founded on this humanism.

Questions concerning today's society are of greater significance than issues of the past. It is more important to reform the faults in people by exposing them, than to engage in titillating and entertaining aestheticism. Babasaheb believed that everyday context, ideas and feelings embedded in social interaction should be predominant in literature.

To Babasaheb, his books were dearer than even his children:

> I cannot understand how time goes while writing books. All my energies are concentrated at the time of writing. I do not care for food. Sometimes I stay up all night to read and write. I am never bored then, nor do I feel boredom. I become very discouraged and dissatisfied as soon as the work is finished. I get the same pleasure when my book is published as I would on having four sons. (Ambedkar 1947)

Babasaheb valued literature that was realistic and life-affirming. This is proved by his love of books, his expectation of humanistic ideas in literature, and his literary thought, which is based on the writer's commitment to common humanity.

4.6 AMBEDKARISM AND DALIT LITERATURE

Ambedkar accorded the highest place to humanism. Inspired by him, Dalit literature holds the human being to be its focal point. This literature is a declaration of human freedom. It encourages human liberation, believes in the greatness of human beings, and firmly opposes notions of race, religion and caste. Humanity is the religion of Dalit literature. Therefore, in its world, no imaginary or worldly object is greater than the human being. It rebels against any culture, society or literature that degrades the human being. Dalit literature will have to be analyzed in the context of the Ambedkarite thought system, of which rebellion is an indivisible part.

4.6.1 Discussions and Lectures Related to Dalit Literature

Dalit literature conferences began to be held from 2 March 1958. Dalit literature has evolved through events such as Buddhist literature conferences, Dalit literature conferences, Dalit theatre conferences, Asmitadarsh festivals, as well as district- and division-level Dalit literature conferences, seminars, book festivals, and Dalit writers' speeches, get-togethers and exchanges.

A great deal of writing about Dalit literature has been published in special issues on Dalit literature, festschrifts and Dalit magazines. Edited collections of thought-provoking speeches by scholars – delivered at different Dalit literature conferences, seminars and festivals – have been published. These collections contain hard-to-find lectures about Dalit literature: *Dr. Babasaheb Ambedkar Preraneche Sahitya* (1977) edited by Bhausaheb Adsul, *Dalit Sahitya: Ek Abhyas* (1978) edited by Arjun Dangle, *Akhil Bharatiya Dalit Sahitya Sammelan: Adhyakshiya Bhashan* (1991) edited by Waman Nimbalkar, *Dalit Sahitya* (1991) edited by Sharankumar Limbale, and *Dalit Sahitya: Charcha ani Chintan* (1993) edited by Gangadhar

Pantawane. Besides these, two books that have proved significant to the journey of Dalit literature are *Dalit Sahitya: Pravah ani Pratikriya* (1986) edited by G M Kulkarni, and *Dalit Sahitya: Ek Samajik Sanskritik Abhyas* (1992) edited by Vidyadhar Pundalik and G M Kulkarni. These collections clarify the form and purpose of Dalit literature in the context of the Ambedkarite world view. They include presidential addresses delivered at various conferences, which put forward unique ideas about Dalit literature. Also, the Dalit writers and savarna critics who figure in these collections have outlined their position vis-à-vis Dalit literature. Baburao Bagul's presidential address at the Buddhist Literature Conference (1971, Mahad), Raja Dhale's presidential address at the Raupya Mahotsavi Buddhist Literature Conference (1973, Mumbai), Namdeo Dhasal's presidential address at the tenth Asmitadarsh Festival (1984, Nagpur), Shankarrao Kharat's presidential address at the All India Dalit Literature Conference (1984, Jalgaon), and Raosaheb Kasbe's address at the All India Dalit Literature Conference (1987, Sholapur)—offer fundamental analyses of the form and purpose of Dalit literature.

There has been an increase in experimentation in Dalit literature, because of the forewords to books on Dalit literature. These are useful in understanding Dalit literature. The forewords – by M N Wankhede for Baburao Bagul's little novel named *Sud* (1970), by Vijay Tendulkar for Namdeo Dhasal's poetry collection, *Tuhi Yatta Kanchi* (1981), and by Narhar Kurundkar for Janardhan Wagmare's volume, *American Negro Wangmay: Samaj ani Sanskriti* (1978) – have proved significant in the discussion of Dalit literature. A few collections of important forewords have also been published. These include, for example, Narhar Kurundkar's *Bhajan* (1981), Gangadhar Pantawane's *Chaitya* (1990), and Yashwant Manohar's *Ambedkari Aswadak Samiksha* (1991). The foreword written by Raja Dhale for Yogiraj Waghmare's story collection, *Gudadani* (1983), is also extremely significant.

On 16 and 24 November 1967, a seminar was held on the topic of 'The Conflict of Culture in Contemporary Maharashtra and the Creative Problem'. Thinkers like M N Wankhede,

W L Kulkarni, R G Jadhav, M P Rege and M B Chitnis participated in the discussions. This seminar could be called the originary event of Dalit criticism. The discussions cast a clear light on the nature and characteristics of the criticism of Dalit literature. Participants presented their views keeping in mind the objections and reservations of writers belonging to the neo-Buddhist community.

In the seminar, Chitnis brought up the important topic of 'socio-anthropological approach' for discussion. Chitnis argued that, unlike African American critics, recent critics of Dalit literature had not used this approach in their analysis. Other participants responded that the application of such an approach in African American literature was a different matter—Blacks and Whites have different heredities, but there is no such difference between Dalits and savarnas. Babasaheb Ambedkar drew on popular and solid arguments to present the thesis that Shudras were Aryan people in works like *Who Were the Shudras? How they came to be the Fourth Varna in the Indo-Aryan Society* (1946), and *The Untouchables: Who were they and Why they became Untouchables?* (1948).

Chitnis contended that though there had been discussion about using a socio-anthropological approach in the context of Dalit literature, there had been no actual analysis based on this approach. There was a dearth of literary creation in the early days of Dalit literature. As a result, the material features of Dalit literature remained the focus of analysis. However, there was scant direct literary basis for Chitnis' proposition. The nature of the discussion initiated by him was suspect, for it was based on conjecture, without direct evidence from early Dalit literature. The debate caused an uproar.

4.6.2 Review of Dalit Literature in Newspapers and Magazines

In newspapers, discussion of Dalit literature appeared in the form of reviews and essays. The first review essay on Dalit literature was 'Dalit Sahityache Samalochan', written by Appasaheb Ranapise in the *Janata* (12 September 1953), a weekly started by Babasaheb Ambedkar. To publish Dalit literature, Dalit writers launched little magazines such as *Aamhi, Nikay, Jatak, Kondi, Sinshagarjana, Sugawa, Asmitadarsh, Dalit Kranti, Sansad, Samaj, Vidroh, Astitwa, Prameya* and *Samuchit*. Besides these, a considerable amount of reviews were featured in the issues of Marathi little magazines, Sunday supplements of newspapers and special issues of magazines on Dalit literature.

The nature of these writings is judgmental, and Dalit writers have objected to them. The book reviewer is on terms of familiarity with the writer, and is often constrained from making a clear and forthright assessment. The reviewer avoids evaluating a book when the review is likely to hurt certain people, and the book is not reviewed properly. The prestige of the venue of publication also affects reviews. In newspapers, editors arrange for reviews to be written according to their preference. They pay more attention to the amount of column space that a piece will occupy, rather than to its substance. People who have not given due thought to Dalit literature write reviews. These reviews tend to be merely introductory, and do not offer in-depth analyses. Firstly, these are brief pieces; secondly, their intent is contaminated by a great deal of prejudice, or, they demonstrate incomplete familiarity with the work. Readers of opinions printed in newspapers often have not yet read the book, and they could be deterred by a biased review.

Books about Dalit literature by Dalit writers also include articles previously published in newspapers, reviews and prefaces: for example, *Dalit Sahityachi Prakash-Yatra* (1980), and *Dr. Ambedkar ani Dalit Sahitya* (1989), written by Bhalchandra Phadke. Dalit commentators have not approached the publication of their collections of reviews with due seriousness. It is as if they handed over their journalistic review articles 'as-is' (i.e. not revised for a different audience) for publication. Consequently, the reviewing of Dalit literature does not appear to have achieved an exemplary standing.

4.6.3 Neglect of the Literary Characteristics of Dalit Literature

Because Dalit literature narrates experiences that have not been heard or seen until now, the reader is shaken while reading them. To the middle-class critic, these experiences appear unprecedented. Therefore, while experiences delineated in Dalit literature are endlessly discussed, the entirety of the artistic creation is cast aside. It is wrong even to expect that middle-class critics will review Dalit literature with any depth. It is not possible for them to fully absorb the experiences of Dalit writers. Insightful consideration of Dalit literature is not possible without fully comprehending factors such as the nature, intensity, language, context and expression of the Dalit writers' caste experience.

The experience delineated in Dalit literature must be viewed objectively, but many Dalit critics are swept away by it. M B Chitnis says:

> I am associated with many SC/ST students. One of them is now doing a PhD. Until the age of twelve he was not familiar with a single letter of the alphabet. He used to cut dead animals, collect money thrown on corpses. At a very young age, his father had taught him to drink liquor. How powerful will it be if he were to write his life. (Chitnis 1998, 53)

It is his stance that Dalits should write about such experiences. This point of view appears to privilege the shock element in Dalit literature. Not to have knowledge of the alphabet till the age of twelve, to drink alcohol at this young age, to skin dead animals, to pick coins off dead bodies—these are frightening experiences. For Chitnis, the recounting of such episodes seems purposeful. However, his position should be interpreted as viewing Dalit life from a middle-class perspective.[4]

---

4. Translator's note: Limbale here appears to contradict himself, since earlier, in responding to Sonwane's question, he had said that the purpose of Dalit literature was indeed to expose the humiliating experiences of Dalit life. However, the contradiction is only apparent. While Limbale objects to Sonwane's question as incongruous, he also rejects Chitnis' position as (*contd.*)

Dalit critics review Dalit literature from a sociological perspective, valuing its revolt against and rejection of exploitation and inequality. However, a literary analysis of the revolt and the rejection in this literature is not undertaken. The social causes of pain, revolt and rejection are analyzed, but the literary form through which these are revealed is not described. Dalit criticism seems more inclined to contemplating the social system than to paying attention to the literary questions. The primary intent of Dalit criticism until now has been to engage in a humanistic evaluation. Ambedkarite thought forms the humanistic thrust of Dalit literature.

4.7 THE ROLE OF DALIT CRITICS IN THE CRITICISM OF DALIT LITERATURE

Dalit literature is a new literary stream. It is the literary expression of a hitherto boycotted society. Its social, cultural and literary environment is distinct from the intent and discourse of mainstream Marathi literature. This is the reason why many obstacles have appeared in the way of its critical evaluation. The question arises: will the middle-class critic assess this literature properly? This fear troubles Dalit writers. Critics are from the higher strata; they have no knowledge of Dalits' lives because Hindu society is highly stratified. The levels of stratification are complex, like a dense forest. Since the touch, shadow and voice of the Dalit person have been determined to be untouchable, a huge chasm of cultural inequality exists between Dalits and savarnas. How will savarna society and critics be able to grasp the mindset of Dalit and neo-Buddhist writers? It will not do for critics to just become modern and use a liberal-reformist approach when considering a new literary stream like Dalit

---

(*contd.*) representing a middle-class mentality, on the basis that these experiences are not to be narrated merely because of their shock value or to titillate, but because of their power to move and bring about transformation. Literature, as he has said, citing Ambedkar, should be accountable and responsible.

literature. They will have to become one with the soul of Dalit literature, and take into consideration the stresses and tensions in the inner being of Dalits, as well as the mindset of Dalit writers and the Dalit society.

Dalit literature needs influential critics who will make the effort to get to know the language and feelings of Dalit society and identify with it wholeheartedly. They can provide a strong inspiration to Dalit literature. Both the propagandizing critic and the flatterer are fatal in the extreme. They do damage to Dalit literature, either through excessive praise, or through indulging in formality and avoiding an honest appraisal. It is never desirable to falsely praise the writer while ignoring the deficiencies in the creation. Such false criticism is harmful for the writer.

It is also wrong for Dalit writers to think that they must always be praised. They should not be angered by criticism. They should acknowledge the criticism of their writing, and introspect. Critics, too, should write unconcerned about angry reactions, or for greed, and writers should welcome honest criticism. This would be true literary conduct. Writers should desist from considering themselves blessed upon receiving accolades or recognition from savarnas; and should not engage in breast-beating on failing to achieve these.

Dalit writers must write for Dalit people, and not hanker after recognition by savarna writers. For healthy growth in their work, it is essential that Dalit writers turn their face to life rather than to criticism. The empathy of Dalits and their awakening are of greater importance than the approval of savarna writers. The act of writing from a life-affirming stance is the Ambedakrism of Dalit literature.

Critics are not in the business of nurturing new writers. The new intellectual critics, especially, prefer setting up camps to being empathetic. Those possessing ideas, mindset and nature similar to theirs gain entry into these cliques. Today's critics have no desire to leave their cliques. On the contrary, they shower high praise on those Dalit writers who are in their factions, and shun those who are not. While one writer may be praised to the skies, another – a good writer – is destroyed by being ignored.

A variety of opinions has been put forward regarding the development of Dalit literature. It has been said that there is a need to search for and build a literary tradition that will have a positive and inspirational impact. Some have expressed the view that, alongside Dalit literature, a body of intellectual literature should also be created. Yet others have felt the necessity to undertake a clear analysis of the emerging tendencies in Dalit literature. And there are those who have demanded that Dalit literature be evaluated *as* literature, with attention being paid to its characteristics and shortcomings. Finally, critics have looked for the possibility of an independent aesthetics of Dalit literature, on the basis of clues derived from an examination of actual literary creations.

4.8 CONCLUSION

The creation of Dalit literature began with the religious conversion of Babasaheb Ambedkar. With his demise soon after the conversion, splits developed among Dalit writers, just as they did in the Dalit movement. In order that Buddhism may expand among Dalits, promoters of the Buddhist world view opposed Dalit literature and supported neo-Buddhist literature. Over time, Dalit writers emerged from the many Dalit castes, sub-castes and tribes. All these writers were Hindus who had not converted to Buddhism.

Neo-Buddhist thinkers were eager that the literature produced following the mass conversion must be Buddhist. But allowance, of time, should be made for the emergence of neo-Buddhist literary creations, since it is not possible for a single generation to give complete shape to any literature. Besides this, neo-Buddhist writers, instead of creating Buddhist literature, became obsessed with a partisan and aggressive condemnation of Dalit literature. Dalit writers and critics undertook a deconstructive and reconstructive discussion of Dalit literature, and established its flow. That is to say, on one hand, they engaged in a serious and honest critique of the emerging literature, and, on the other, developed the benchmarks for the form and purpose of a powerful and relevant Dalit literature. Writers from many Dalit castes, sub-castes, tribes and Adivasi groups enriched Dalit literature with original creations. This was no longer exclusively the literature of neo-Buddhist writers. As a result, discussion of literature based on the Buddhist thought system fell behind.

Critical writing on Dalit literature commenced side by side with the emergence of Dalit literature. Consequently, this critical writing could hardly base itself on a concrete body of literature. On this account, criticism in the early period was suspect, and a large part of it was made up of newspaper reviews. These reviews mainly consisted of brief introductions, and opinions and comments on the texts. Dalit writers and critics lent their support because they wanted to establish this new literary stream called Dalit literature. This was the reason why their writing was filled with sentiments of approval, reverence, curiosity and praise. Dalit as well as savarna critics participated in the discussion of Dalit literature from the very beginning. The presidential addresses of various Dalit literature conferences constitute another kind of criticism. In these presidential speeches, Dalit literature has been assessed in terms of its values and commitments. They have been helpful in clarifying the form, purpose, characteristics and role of Dalit literature. In a true sense, the presidential addresses constitute the preamble to Dalit literature.

5

Dalit Literature and Marxism

5.1 INTRODUCTION

If there is one trend in Dalit literature that systematically opposes
Marxism, there is another that seeks convergence between the
thoughts of Marx and Ambedkar. What was Babasaheb
Ambedkar's position in relation to Marxism? What is the
relationship between Marxism and Dalit literature? Is it possible
to discuss Marxist literature and the Marxist movement along
with Dalit literature and the Dalit movement? It seems
important to study these questions in depth.

5.2 MARXISM, AND THE SHORTCOMINGS
OF INDIAN MARXISM

Karl Marx expanded on Hegel's principle of 'dialectical progress'.
He gave fuller shape to the concept of dialectical progress, and
demonstrated that its essence operates in inanimate objects,
social relations, as well as human history. The crux of dialectical
progress is that, in no sphere does progress occur until its old
form is destroyed. Marxism is based on dialectical progress and
'historical materialism'. According to Marxism, history until the
present day is the history of conflict between classes, which were
formed because of relations of production. The materialism
propounded by Marx holds that social conditions change due
to systems of production, relations of production and class
conflict. The core principle of historical materialism is that
religion, ethics, art, literature and culture are inspired by
economic forces.

Marx proposed the theory of surplus value, and demonstrated how labour is exploited under capitalism. The capitalist compensates the worker for six hours, but extracts twelve hours of work, thus obtaining six hours of free labour. This free labour turns into surplus value, which is appropriated and accumulated by the capitalist while the exploitation of workers continues.

Karl Marx and Friedrich Engels published *The Communist Manifesto* in 1848. The *Manifesto* describes the formation of a communist society. It declares that all workers must unite in a revolution to end the capitalist social system. In order to destroy capitalism, Marx even advocated a violent class war. Further, Marx and Engels said that following the workers' revolution, and until the emergence of an exploitation-free, classless society, a dictatorship of the proletariat will be necessary for a period. *The Communist Manifesto* declared that in the communist society, the right to private property will be destroyed, hereditary rights will be extinguished, the treasury will be nationalized and, putting an end to private ownership of transportation, all rights will be vested in the state.

In other words, Marxism is the ideology of the exploited. The fundamental credo of Marxism is the merciless crushing of the cruel exploitation unleashed by the privileged, and the achievement of full justice for the exploited who have no rights. The goal of Marxism is the creation of a society that is exploitation-free and classless.

Marx and Engels were the originators of Marxism, and Lenin contributed to its development. In the USSR, many new ideas were incorporated into Marxism after Stalin. Nikita Khruschev launched a campaign against Stalin's unbridled state. In China, Mao Zedong and his comrades proposed the concept of a 'workers' state'. Mikhail Gorbachev announced economic reforms and *glasnost* in the USSR. Boris Yeltsin made a declaration of individual freedom and ended the rule of the Communist Party. Western Marxist philosophers also added new ideas. But Indian Marxists do not seem to have made any contribution to the development of Marxism by examining it in the context of the Hindu social system. Marxists did not pay any real attention to the issue of untouchability. If they had done so, there would have been a creative development of Marxism consistent with Indian conditions.

Socialists laid stress on political and economic struggles. In order to realize the goal of social revolution, it was essential to link this struggle with the cultural struggle—which the socialists did not. Indian Marxist thought would have developed if the communist movement had been organized around social, educational and cultural questions. Marxists in India waged struggles on workers' issues, but they paid no attention to the caste system and untouchability. Hence Marxists failed to earn the trust of the Dalits.

Marxism must develop in the context of Indian social conditions. Marx offered an excellent analysis of the organization of the village in India. New ideas will have to be formulated by linking this analysis to the caste system, religion and ethics. Indian Marxism cannot evolve without taking into consideration the unequal social order created by Hinduism, because inequality in Indian society is not the consequence of capitalism alone. It is a much more complex disparity, and there can be no movement forward unless the place of caste, morality and truth in Hinduism is evaluated. A common battle will have to be fought on both social and economic fronts. In this regard, Marxism will need to: first, prepare peasants and workers for an economic struggle; second, include other social groups in a mass movement; and third, broaden and deepen the process of social awakening.

Since Marx's thought appears incomplete in the context of the Indian social system it must be developed with reference to it.

5.3   DR AMBEDKAR'S POSITION ON INDIAN MARXISM

Babasaheb Ambedkar's life and work were dedicated to the well-being of those whom society had boycotted. He thought about religion, economy, literature, politics, society, law and freedom in terms of the interests of the untouchables. He did not ignore these interests in his consideration of Marxism. While he held that there was neither caste discrimination nor untouchability in communism, he considered Indian Marxism to be incomplete because it did not think about ending caste. The destruction of untouchability was, for him, the paramount concern. Hence, he said, 'If Lenin had been born in Hindustan, he would have first destroyed caste discrimination and untouchability completely; and he would not even have imagined a revolution without this' (Ambedkar 1929b). Or, 'if Tilak had been born in a boycotted caste, instead of roaring, "Swaraj is my birthright", he would have said with confidence, "Annihilation of untouchability is my supreme duty"' (Ambedkar 1927c). From his thoughts on Lenin and Tilak, we can conclude that Babasaheb considered the elimination of caste to be of greater importance than revolution or swaraj. Both revolution and swaraj are politically inspired movements, but, clearly, Babasaheb remained firm in his view that in India, social revolution is more important than political revolution.

India's Hindu society is divided into many castes and sub-castes. This caste system is not based only on a division of society, but also on the existence of a hierarchical notion of superiority. Castes consider each other to be inferior. Each caste looks upon the other with suspicion. If these castes were destroyed, some of them would lose more power and status than others. Consequently, we do not see class consciousness in Hindu society. As Babasaheb said: 'Caste System is not merely a division of labour. *It is also a division of labourers*' (Ambedkar 1989, 47; Ambedkar's emphasis).

Caste system not only divides work, it also divides workers. This division is based on religious rules and the imaginary of high and low. Therefore, the social status of the exploited savarna and the exploited Dalit is not identical. The social divide between a Brahman worker and a Dalit worker should be kept in mind. Babasaheb Ambedkar criticized Communists for ignoring this inequality. He felt that Indian Communists had not taken up cudgels against Brahmanism: 'I have heard labour leaders giving eloquent speeches against capitalism. But I have not heard a single labour leader speak against Brahmanism among workers' (Ambedkar 1938). To him, Brahmanism was as much a conspiracy of exploitation as capitalism. The unequal Hindu system enslaved and exploited the Dalits, and inflicted injustices and ill treatment on them. Babasaheb gave priority to the slaves' struggle against inequality. He criticized labour leaders for not speaking against the cycle of repression perpetrated by Brahmanism. Commenting on the reason why labour leaders did not condemn Brahmanism, he said: 'If Communists' views about god and religion were to be stated openly, they will not find a single follower among workers in today's situation' (Ambedkar 1929b).

In a speech at the Fourth Conference of the World Fellowship of Buddhists in Kathmandu on 20 November 1956, and in his unpublished essay, *Buddha or Karl Marx*, Babasaheb Ambedkar made a comparative assessment of Marx and Buddha. He preferred Buddha's thought because, according to him, Marxism promoted violence and dictatorship. He said that if the Buddha's concept of sorrow was to be considered identical to Marx's theory of exploitation, there was no difference between the two. While Buddha was against violence, he permitted its use where necessary to achieve justice. In Babasaheb's view, the sangha was a model of communism without dictatorship. True, it was communism on a very small scale. Babasaheb believed that humanism needed not only economic values, but spiritual values as well. Therefore, he challenged Communists to demonstrate whether, while pursuing their goals, they had not destroyed any values. He asked, 'How many people did they kill to gain their objective? Did human life have no value?' (Keer 1987, 507–08; Ambedkar 1987, 441, 444, 450, 452). Babasaheb found spiritual values and human life important. He rejected Marxism out of this respect for life.

5.4 MARXISM OR AMBEDKARISM?

The debate on Marxism versus Ambedkarism gained wide currency after Dr Babasaheb Ambedkar's death. On 3 October

1957, the followers of Ambedkar established the Republican Party of India based on his vision. There was tremendous debate and controversy over Marxism among the leaders of the party. Dadasaheb Gaikwad proposed that the Republican Party of India was the party of the dispossessed, the oppressed and the exploited. B C Kamble accused Gaikwad of being a Marxist. Consequently, the party divided into two groups.

On 9 July 1972, an organization of Dalit youth, called Dalit Panthers, emerged from the political failure of the Republican Party of India. It began to work on Dalit questions, as an activist organization of Dalit youth. Marxism became a subject of controversy among the young leaders of the Dalit Panthers as well. The Dalit Panthers' manifesto issued by Namdeo Dhasal was criticized as being Marxist by Raja Dhale. Dhasal had played a major role in preparing this manifesto, called 'Dalit Panthercha Jahirnama,' along with Sunil Dihe, a naxalite activist. He had included the dispossessed, the exploited and the suffering in his definition of Dalits. Raja Dhale did not like this. Calling Dhasal a Communist, Dhale disowned the Dalit Panthers and formed an organization called Mass Movement. As a result, the Dalit Panthers was divided.

Just as Marxism became a major subject of controversy among Dalit leaders and activists, likewise, it became a widespread topic of debate and discussion among Dalit writers and critics. The separate Buddhist, Dalit and Asmitadarsh literary conferences are clear examples of group formation among Dalit writers.

5.4.1 Opposition to Marxism

Dalit writers and critics have demonstrated opposition towards Marxism. Where Marxist ideology of revolution is based only on economic disparity, Ambedkarite ideology is founded on the phenomenon of untouchability underlying social inequality. Since Marxism does not take social disparity into consideration, Dalit critics take the view that Marxist ideology is incomplete.

In their opinion, Marxism does not speak up against social inequality as Ambedkarism does. And therefore, they have concluded that Babasaheb has not spoken against economic disparity. However, they need to understand that neither Marx's nor Ambedkar's thought is so one-dimensional that it should be labeled only economic or only social. It will just not do to say that Dalits' questions are only social, that they have nothing to do with economic issues. Dalits are subject to social as well as economic inequality. They will have to struggle at both levels. As Dalit literature is the literature of Dalits' struggles, it has to be asserted that the Dalit literary movement will have to accept Marxism along with Ambedkarism.

5.4.2 Need for Convergence between Marx and Ambedkar

Those so-called intellectuals who seek a meaningful equation with Dalit literature by taking Marxism out of Ambedkarism or vice versa only delude themselves. If this is not the case, then they are consciously or unwittingly committing literary and societal betrayal.

The focal point of Ambedkarism is the common person. The focus of Marxism also rests on the exploited, suffering common person. The essence of the thoughts of Babasaheb Ambedkar, Karl Marx and Gautama Buddha is the same—the liberation of human beings from exploitation. Given this similarity, it seems that there should be a blending of the thoughts of Marx and Ambedkar. But Raja Dhale does not support this possibility. According to him, it is not true that we are poor therefore we are untouchable. The truth, he believes, is that we are untouchable therefore we are poor. Otherwise, every poor person in India would be untouchable! Rather than the root of our untouchability being in poverty, the root of our poverty lies in our untouchability. In Dhale's analysis, the source of untouchability lies in Indian history and the Hindu religion, and not in present-day capitalism (Dhale 1992).

The poverty and untouchability of Dalits is rooted in history and religion, and from that root has emerged a great tree. Untouchability has been replaced by discrimination based on caste. But it needs to be remembered that this discrimination is not located in history or religion, but in today's politics. Though the origin of Dalits' poverty is in untouchability, it cannot be said this is its only cause. Untouchability is now coming to an end due to transformations in social life brought about by inter-caste marriages, religious conversion, laws, Dalit agitations, progressive ideas, science and technology. However, the demon of caste discrimination is now raising its head, further sharpening the social issues confronting Dalits. Besides, all-pervasive unemployment, corruption, rising population, high costs of living, concentration of the organized production sector and political power in a handful of the rich, deserted villages and increasing number of filthy slums in the cities, have further trampled and oppressed Dalit life. These aspects of current reality cannot be ignored on the basis that they are all rooted in history and religion. We must recognize that the source of such problems are today's inequitable arrangements. The origin of Dalits' poverty may well be in religion and history, but its present face is fundamentally different. Further, Dalit poverty has become a far more complex phenomenon on account of the government's public welfare schemes, reservations and the emergence of a new Dalit middle class.

While the cause of Dalits' economic slavery is hidden in the Indian social order, the ultimate path to liberation will be found only through the convergence of Marxism and Ambedkarism. With the rapid growth of cities due to industrialization, Marxism can give Dalits and savarnas alike knowledge of equal economic relations, as well as inspiration to get organized. A class system is coming into being in the villages with mechanization and the cracks appearing in the caste system due to new land-related laws. However, the fissures appearing in the traditional caste system have not brought an end to caste spirit. While caste spirit has gained strength in society, a class spirit is also on the rise due to the exploitation of the oppressed and the bond of common interest. The growing strength of left-wing ideology in movements and organizing efforts suggests that a class system will take the place of the caste system.

The convergence of Marxism and Ambedkarism is essential for a widespread, popular movement. Proponents of convergence think that the Dalit minority will not be able to fight against the unequal social system single-handedly. The support of labourers and workers who are also experiencing hardship will have to be obtained—this will ease the path of socialism. But Raja Dhale opposes this approach: 'The idea of blending Marx, Phule and Ambedkar is motivated not by a desire to bring glory to Phule and Ambedkar, but by the thought of bringing glory to Marx' (Dhale 1992).

The reason for Raja Dhale's trenchant opposition to Marxism is obvious. However, such opposition is not widespread, and is usually offensive and one-sided. It is born in the heat of asserting a particular position and rebutting another view. The conflicts between White and Black, capitalist and worker, savarna and Dalit, are intended to wrest freedom from slavery. Although every type of slavery has its distinct form, even so, a common spirit of freedom and struggle imbues them all. The struggle of Blacks, workers and Dalits is for justice. Therefore, it seems logical that there should be a convergence of their ideas and movements.

5.4.3 Differences of Opinion among Dalit Writers

Ambedkar's thoughts are the sole inspiration for Dalit literature. Though all Dalit writers recognize this, yet there are obvious differences among them. The first instance of this disagreement was anti-Marxist Buddhism. Having accepted the Buddhist thought system, Bhausaheb Adsul, Vijay Sonwane and Raja Dhale have criticized the writings of Dalit writers such as Baburao Bagul, Namdeo Dhasal and Daya Pawar by calling them Communists. Arjun Dangle, Daya Pawar and Yashwant Manohar advocated a Marxist position for Dalit writers. Subsequently, the point of disagreement changed, and a discussion involving Marxism and Ambedkarism began. Gangadhar Pantawane endorsed Ambedkarism, and claimed that Baburao Bagul and Yashwant Manohar were Marxists. When, concurrently, Raosaheb Kasbe's book *Ambedkar ani Marx* (1985) was published, Kasbe, rather than Bagul, became the target of criticism.

The argument for a synthesis of Marxism and Ambedkarism was strongly presented in books like Kasbe's *Ambedkar ani Marx*, V S Jog's *Marxwad ani Dalit Sahitya* (1985), Sharad Patil's *Abrahmani Sahityache Saundaryashastra* (1988), and Sada Karhwade's *Marxwad, Buddhawad ani Ambedkarwad* (1980). But the Ambedkarites did not make a similar effort to work through the ideas of Marx and Ambedkar. They did not propose an Ambedkarite economic thought as an alternative to Marxist economic thought. They were unsuccessful in giving a scientific Ambedkarite base to the movement, derived from a scientific analysis of Ambedkar's thought. The truth is, this was as far as they could go. Since Babasaheb Ambedkar opposed Marx, the anti-Marxists assumed an oppositional stance. However, they could not develop Ambedkarism on a scientific basis. Eventually, this controversy took a different direction. The discussion among Dalit thinkers began to revolve around Hindutva versus Ambedkarism.

Proponents of Hindutva began to compare Dr Hedgewar with Dr Ambedkar. Dalit writers such as Ramnath Chavan, Babasaheb Gaikwad, Gangadhar Pantawane and Texas Gaikwad went on Hindutva platforms to express their views. As a result, the issue of Hindutva versus Ambedkarism emerged in the discussions. Its most public form was Yashwant Manohar's views against Gangadhar Pantawane. Manohar accused Pantawane of being a Hindutva supporter because of a speech he had made from the platform of Samarsatta Mancha, a Hindutva organization. Ultimately, this controversy plunged to the level of exchanges like, 'Who is the true Ambedkarite—you or I?' Lakshman Mane, Partha Polke, Arjun Dangle, Baburao Bagul, Vilas Wagh and Raosaheb Kasbe took an anti-Hindutva position.

The differences of opinion among Dalit writers were never purely intellectual. Implicit in them were personal jealousies, leadership ambitions and selfish feelings. As a result, the disagreements remained on a personal level, despite shifts of form, centre and target. In newspapers, too, these differences remained confined to topical discussions of passing interest. No serious work reflecting on these disagreements and controversies emerged. They did not achieve the importance and status of intellectual trends.

5.5 MARXIST CRITICISM AND DALIT CRITICISM

If Marxist criticism developed from Marx's and Engels' perspectives on literature, Dalit criticism grew out of Ambedkar's thought. Marx and Engels did not write extensively about either the form or theory of art. Their position on literature has to be inferred from their writings, which is also true of Babasaheb Ambedkar. Many similarities are evident between Marxist literary criticism and Dalit literary criticism.

5.5.1 Basis for the Two Schools of Criticism

Both Marxist criticism and Dalit criticism have emerged from particular intellectual locations. Developed in the context of historical materialism, Marxist literary criticism offers certain definite conclusions about human life, and an outline of the possibility of progress. Because Marxism is a humanist thought with a vision for forming an exploitation-free society, Marxist literary criticism is founded on an egalitarian philosophy of life. Given this intellectual base, its ideas on the form and purpose of art are expressed with clarity. In this context, it is useful to look at Maxim Gorky's address on Soviet literature to the first All-Union Congress of Soviet Writers, on 17 August 1934. He reminded his audience of 'Engels's most valuable statement: "Our [Marx, Engels and Lenin's] theory is not a credo but a guide to action."' For Gorky, this meant that literary criticism, instead of taking 'recourse to unvarying quotations from Marx, Engels and Lenin,' must proceed 'from the facts provided by an immediate observation of the rapid march of life, when it gives appraisals of themes, characters and human relationships' (Gorky 1982, 339–40).

Daya Pawar assumed a position quite similar to that of Gorky. While recognizing the thought of Marx, Engels and Lenin as the essence of communist literature, he says that writers must reflect on how best to express the idea of freedom from exploitation in literature. He believes that the ideas of Phule, Ambedkar and Marx can help Dalit writers see their own exploitation clearly (Pawar 1990, 77).

5.5.2 Motivated Literary Criticism

Marxist as well as Dalit literary criticisms are inspired by definite ideas, just as their respective literatures are. The thoughts of Marx and Ambedkar are geared towards human freedom. The works inspired by these thought systems are marked by commitment. In regard to the purpose of communist literature, Gorky says:

> Truths are created by socially useful labour with the supreme aim of building up a classless society in which the physical energy expended wastefully by man will turn into intellectual energy, and in which unlimited opportunities will be given to the development of an individual's abilities and talents. The task of literature is to portray this working life and to embody the truths in images—characters and types. (Gorky 1982, 307)

Communist art is needed to prepare people for revolution. As Gorky, citing Engels, says in his talk with young Soviet writers, 'Friedrich Engels, a wise man, said that ... all our actions, when summed up, are aimed at changing the old world, and creating a new one' (Gorky 1982, 295). Ambedkar takes a similar position with respect to Dalit literature: 'There must be writing in a society on the verge of revolution, because it is necessary to take to people those ideas whose inspirational power prepares a society for revolution' (Khandekar 1981, 8).

Both Marxist and Dalit writers take the side of the exploited. The function of both literatures is to make people conscious of their slavery. Therefore, the task of criticism is to assess whether or not the necessary knowledge is developed through these literatures. This criticism demands that these literatures express creative desire, a decisive outcome for the struggle, courage and other revolutionary qualities.

5.5.3   Committed Literary Criticism

Both Marxist and Dalit literatures and literary criticisms are life-affirming, even though their paths are independent and distinct. Marxist literature is a literature of realism, and so is Dalit literature. It does not appear that these literatures will be trapped in the aesthetic of entertainment. In fact, Dalit literature is created from reality and experience. Life-affirmation pervades Dalit literature, even if the specific term is not used. There is little affirmation of life in the works of middle-class writers of Marathi literature. The humanism of Marathi literature seems to circle around questions related to child marriage, re-marriage, widow marriage, marriage in old age, love marriage, divorce, wives' faithfulness, difficult widowhood, women's education, prohibition and the dowry system. The creators of Dalit literature have to take on the historic task of contributing the best life-affirming ideas to Indian literature. Marx and Engels recognized realism to be the finest achievement of world art. Dalit literature too rejects aestheticism and embraces humanism.

5.5.4   Recognition of Artistic Values

Though Marxist and Dalit literatures reject aestheticism, they do not underestimate the value of art. In a letter to Minna Kautsky on 26 November 1885, Engels said:

> I am not at all an opponent of tendentious poetry as such ... But I think that the bias should flow by itself from the situation and action, without particular indications, and that the writer is not obliged to obtrude on the reader the future historical solutions of the social conflicts pictured ... [A] socialist-biased novel fully achieves its purpose, in my view, if by conscientiously describing the real mutual relations, breaking down conventional illusions about them, it shatters the optimism of the bourgeois world, instills doubt as to the eternal character of the existing order, although the author

does not offer any definite solution or does not even line up openly on any particular side. (Marx and Engels 1947, 45)

Clearly, Marxism does not approve of an openly propagandist form of literature. It does not consider literature to be just a medium of propaganda, but as a form of art, something to be cultivated. With respect to Dalit literature, Yashwant Manohar says, 'The literature that achieves a unique unification of the finest values of life and of art will in future be recognized as Dalit literature. The radical view of art thus created will be the highest glory of Marathi literary history' (Manohar 1978, 69). Manohar's position regarding the unification of the values of life and art resembles that of Engels.

5.5.5 The Human Being is the Finest Value

Marxist literature and Dalit literature alike believe in the greatness of the common human being—a belief that has been conveyed in criticism as well. Marxism is humanistic, and, for it, the human being is the centre of art and life. Maxim Gorky says:

> We must realize that it is the masses' labour that is the chief organizer of culture and the creator of all ideas, those that have for ages detracted from the decisive significance of labour—that source of all our knowledge, as well as the ideas of Marx, Lenin and Stalin, which are instilling a revolutionary consciousness of their rights in proletarians of all lands, and in our country are elevating labour to a force that is the basis of creativeness in science and art. (Gorky 1982, 332)

It is the reverent belief of Dalit writers that in this world no imaginary or otherworldly object can be greater than the human being. Since both Dalit and Marxist literatures have focused on the human being, there is a perceptible similarity in the inspiration, role and commitment of these literatures. This has been especially stated in Marxist and Dalit literary criticisms.

5.5.6 The Common Man is the Hero

The common man is the protagonist of both Dalit and Marxist literatures. This is a new protagonist. In the work of established writers, this protagonist had been ground under. They did not see heroes among ordinary people. As A Leizerov says of the works of Gorky:

> In the works of Maxim Gorky, the father of socialist realism, life was seen for the first time through the eyes of the class to which the future belonged—the working class. In his works ... people began to be portrayed already not so much as a spontaneous force but rather as the conscious maker of history. The new heroes, the workers, shown to the world of Maxim Gorky, were not like their predecessors in classical literature; for example, not like the unfortunate toilers deserving of compassion in Dickens, the loners, enlighteners-utopians in Georges Sand, or the people blinded by hate and beaten by life in Zola or in Kuprin's novel *Moloch*. In paving the way for the literature of the future, Gorky showed how new people who knew how to rebuild the world were moulded in the fire of revolutionary struggle. (Leizerov 1976, 157–58)

Baburao Gaekwad expresses a similar view about Dalit literature: 'People of every caste and religion were involved in the fight for the country, but the untouchable person being of inferior status never became a hero. Therefore, Dalits were not portrayed in modern Marathi literature' (Gaekwad 1986, 38).

Dalit and Marxist literatures made the exploited human being – who had been unknown until then – their protagonist. Dalit and Marxist criticisms established and elaborated on the role of this new hero, and thus gave it support. Promoting the liberation of the common man, this criticism made a strong attack on the exploiter's art, literature, society, culture, economy and politics.

Dalit literature and Marxist literature are motivated by definite aims and thoughts. Consequently, there is resemblance in their form and purpose. Both derive their inspiration, role and commitment from humanism. In both thoughts, literatures, movements and societies, the idea of the common man's freedom and greatness has been expressed. Despite differences of country, state, language and conditions, the unity that is evident in Dalit and Marxist literatures derives from sentiments of revolt against exploitation, support for human liberation, and respect for the greatness of humanity.

5.6 MARXIST–AMBEDKARITE CRITICISM

Dalit literature has been critiqued from Marxist and Ambedkarite perspectives from the very beginning. Progressive writers and critics have made an important intervention in the developmental phase of Dalit literature. Intellectuals like P S Nerurkar, G B Sardar, Sharatchandra Muktibodh, Narhar Kurundkar, Sudhir Bedekar, Sharad Patil, Narayan Surve, Sada Karhade and V S Jog have supported Dalit literature; Marxists and socialists have expressed confidence in it. M N Wankhede, Baburao Bagul, Yashwant Manohar, Raosaheb Kasbe, Arjun Dangle, Namdeo Dhasal and Daya Pawar, for example, accepted Marxism in their consideration of Dalit literature.

5.6.1 A Class-based Definition of the Word 'Dalit'

Not only are the scheduled castes and sub-castes Dalit, all exploited are also Dalit, according to the definition given by Marxist commentators. M N Wankhede says: 'Not only are the Buddhist or the backward defined by the word Dalit, but whoever are exploited workers, all of them are also included in the definition of "Dalit"' (Wankhede 1981, 78). Namdeo Dhasal has offered a similar definition: 'Dalits are the scheduled castes, sub-castes, Buddhists, working masses, labourers, landless farm workers, yayawars and adivasis' (Dhasal 1973). Wankhede and Dhasal included all the powerless sectors of society in their definitions of who is Dalit. These definitions are constructed from feelings of comprehensive social and political unity. In fact, these are not just definitions, but also a kind of call to action, to prepare for struggles. All those sections of society who are marked by social, economic and cultural exploitation are Dalit. The caste of those who are exploited is 'exploited'.

Wankhede and Dhasal addressed the exploited as Dalit. But such a broad definition was unacceptable to the opponents of Marxism. The generally accepted definition of the word Dalit pertains to the root sense of belonging to untouchable and nomadic communities. This should not mean that the definitions given by Wankhede and Dhasal are less important. In terms of broad social and political unity, these are very important for social awakening and organizing. The language of 'Bahujanwad' that is heard so loudly in today's Indian society and political life is to be found in these definitions. If we consider Dalit literature to be a movement, then the position of Wankhede and Dhasal seems appropriate in terms of broader interest and direction.

5.6.2 Dalit Consciousness and Class Consciousness

Marx and Engels said in *The German Ideology*, 'Life is not determined by consciousness, but consciousness by life' (Marx and Engels 1947, 13). That is, consciousness is formed by the same conditions that form the human being. It is, therefore, important to deliberate on Dalit consciousness and class consciousness. Sharatchandra Muktibodh says, 'Relative to Dalit consciousness, Marxist consciousness is fundamentally different' (Muktibodh 1986, 96). Vasant Palsikar has differentiated between Dalit consciousness and class consciousness: 'Class-consciousness and Dalit consciousness are different. Dalit consciousness militates against unity' (Palsikar 1986, 118). Palsikar has even argued that Dalit consciousness can hurt class consciousness. It nurtures caste consciousness, as a result of which it becomes injurious, bitter and aggressive. As caste-based feeling becomes intense and aggressive, all people from other castes appear as enemies, whether or not they belong to a dominant community. It is Palsikar's analysis that is fundamentally flawed in equating Dalit consciousness with caste consciousness. Dalit consciousness is a revolutionary consciousness motivated by the desire for freedom from slavery. Its inspiration is Ambedkarite thought on ending caste, rather than a caste spirit. The literature of all Dalit castes and sub-castes is recognized as Dalit literature. Not all writers from the different castes and sub-castes are inspired in their writing by a consciousness of self-identity. They write with the objective of destroying an inequitable system.

That Dalit consciousness is only opposed to the caste system and Marxist consciousness is only opposed to capitalism is an inappropriate distinction. As Marxist consciousness is produced by a capitalist situation, so is Dalit consciousness engendered by a Brahmanical context. Therefore, it is useless to complain that Marxism does not speak against Brahmanism or that Dalit consciousness does not speak against capitalism. It is self-evident that the two are the products of different circumstances. But this does not mean that they are entirely distinct or mutually damaging. Both Marxist and Dalit consciousnesses rebel against the particular circumstances that produced them, and both are opposed to inequality. Their battlefields are different; however, their objective is the same, namely, the liberation of human beings.

Just as a nation's army fights against the alien enemy-nation on many fronts, so do these consciousnesses. The same army can fight for the nation while scattered on many fronts. It should be recognized that the consciousnesses engaged in the continuing battle against inequality in different parts of the world, though dispersed, are fighting for humanism the world over. Dalit consciousness is distinct from Marxist consciousness and Black consciousness; the sites of their battle are different, yet their final aim is human liberation. This demonstrates how the consciousnesses against inequality operative in the struggles going on in various parts of the world complement one another.

5.6.3 The Dalit Question is not only Social

The Dalit question is not only social, it is economic as well. The economic aspect of the Dalit question cannot be dismissed.

Today, untouchables are ill-treated, and the chief cause of their ill treatment is their economic powerlessness. In order to survive, they have to depend on a sector of society that guards its self-interest. A large section of today's Dalits are landless farm-workers, they have no means of their own to produce goods or engage in business. Until they are able to stand on their own feet, they will be compelled to take up dirty jobs. They will have to fight strongly against economic as well as social inequity. That is, they will have to simultaneously fight a class war and a caste war. How are Dalits to be freed not only from the caste system but also from economic inequality? Dalits are not just untouchable, they are poor too. Their untouchability must end, and their poverty along with it. Dalits' slavery will not end with the destruction of untouchability—for this, class struggle is important.

5.6.4 Marx and Ambedkar Compared

The caste system existed for thousands of years. The occupation of each caste was unalterable, and each had carried on the same occupation for generations. No attempt was made to search for new ways and modes of living. New knowledge and new technology arrived with the advent of the British in India, and these weakened the caste system.

Untouchables obtained education and entry into the military because of the British. They also entered service as labourers in ports, railways, and telegraph and postal services. Consequently, their traditional occupations changed and new questions arose. Along with social questions, economic questions assumed critical proportions for Dalits. Since the particular focus of Dalit movements had been on social struggles for self-respect, the economic questions had remained unanswered. Dadasaheb Gaekwad organized a mass movement for the landless. Dalit Panthers agitated for land awards. These campaigns proved to be too far removed from, and too little for, the increasing economic pressure faced by Dalits. The Dalit Panthers struggled for fifteen long years to get the Marathwada University renamed after Dr Babasaheb Ambedkar. As a result, they could not pay attention to economic issues. Because of groupism and power politics in the Republican Party of India, the party's leadership did not give these issues the necessary attention either. Consequently, the economic problems of Dalits worsened. The argument for the convergence of Marxist and Ambedkarite ideologies was put forward. Simultaneously, opposition to the growing influence of Marxism on Dalit literature and the Dalit movement also began to be expressed.

There are many commonalities between Dalit and Marxist literatures. The most prominent likeness is the centrality of the human being in both literatures. Both literatures are life-affirming, and adhere to realism. To a large extent, the stance of the Dalit writer is similar to that of the Marxist writer. The Marxist writer imagines the end of exploitative capitalism in order to destroy economic inequity. The Dalit writer envisions the end of the caste system in order to eradicate social inequity. The Marxist writer believes that human beings should be free from exploitation. The Dalit writer holds that people should be free from degradation, and be able to live as humans. Both want all avenues to be open for human beings to attain greatness, and both have voiced revolt against exploitation. Marxist and Dalit writers write out of a commitment to oppose inequality.

The common man is central to the thoughts of Marx, Ambedkar and Buddha. All three seek to free human beings from exploitation. This is underscored in Raosaheb Kasbe's *Ambedkar ani Marx*, Sharad Patil's *Abramhaniya Sahityache Saundaryashastra*, and Sada Karhade's *Marxvad, Buddhavad ani Ambedkarvad*. Dalits cannot turn down the participation of exploited workers, if they wish to engage in total revolution. A single caste or sub-caste, a single religion or sect, a single province or a few groups in a province cannot accomplish this task. To achieve this revolution, there has to be a convergence of the anti-caste Ambedkarite thought and the anti-class Marxist thought.

During the same period that there was extensive debate around Marx and Ambedkar in the Dalit movement and Dalit literature, the so-called Gandhi versus Ambedkar debate also came to the fore. The differences and similarities between the thoughts of Babasaheb Ambedkar and Mahatma Gandhi have been explored in Ratnakar Ganvir's *Gandhi ani Ambedkar: Teen Mulakhati* (1983), G B Sardar's *Gandhi ani Ambedkar* (1987), and Alim Vakil's *Bodhisatva ani Mahatma* (1990). Intellectuals like Vasant Palsikar, Madhu Limaye and Nalini Pandit have written comprehensively and creatively on the question of Gandhi and Ambedkar.

Followers of Gandhi, such as G B Sardar, P L Deshpande, G P Pradhan, V S Khandekar and S M Joshi, have helped Dalit literature. The debates on Marx and Ambedkar, and Gandhi and Ambedkar, have taken place also because of Babasaheb Ambedkar's own opposition to Marx and Gandhi. However, the thoughts of Marx and Gandhi, along with those of Ambedkar, have proved fundamental to the development of Dalit literature.

5.7　CONCLUSION

Babasaheb Ambedkar criticized Indian Communists because they did not fight against the caste system. He preferred Buddhist thought, which promoted democracy and non-violence, and rejected Marx's thought, because Marx accepted the use of violence in the struggle against capitalism. Believing that Marxist thought was incomplete as far as the Indian situation was concerned, Indian Marxist thinkers adopted, after Babasaheb's death and in response to the criticisms, a perspective that would enable the development of a Marxism consistent with the Indian social context. Thinkers like Karhade, Manohar, Patil and Jog saw the possibility of a positive relationship in the thoughts of Phule, Ambedkar and Marx.

Dalit issues are not only social; they are economic as well. It becomes apparent from a serious examination of the caste system that a very powerful, inequitable economic system is functioning behind it. Dalit minorities on their own will not be able to destroy this entrenched unequal system. Those who accept the thoughts of Marx as well as Ambedkar have argued that, for this unequal system to be annihilated, there needs to be a meeting of Ambedkar's anti-caste thought and Marx's anti-class thought. Prominent among these are M N Wankhede, Baburao Bagul, Namdeo Dhasal, Daya Pawar, Arjun Dangle, Yashwant Manohar, Raosaheb Kasbe, Sharad Patil, Sada Karhade, Narayan Surve, Sudhir Bedekar, Sharatchandra Muktibodh, P S Nerurkar and V S Jog. Among those opposed to this point of view are Bhausaheb Adsul, Raja Dhale, Vijay Sonwane, R G Jadhav, Harish Khanderao, Gangadhar Pantawane and Sudhakar Gaekwad.

Similarities between the form and purpose of Dalit and Marxist literatures exist due to the particular aims and ideas inspiring them—specifically their commitment to humanism. While Dalit writers have called this humanism by the name of Ambedkarism, Marxist writers have named it Marxism. Ideas of human freedom and greatness have been articulated in both thoughts, literatures, movements and societies. Despite differences of country, province, language and conditions, both rebel against exploitation, support the freedom of human beings, and respect the greatness of common people.

In the period following Babasaheb Ambedkar's death, intellectual debates have taken place in the name of Marx versus Ambedkar, and Gandhi versus Ambedkar. It is evident that while Ambedkar's thought is the main intellectual current underlying the criticism of Dalit literature, other progressive ideas have also entered into it.

6

Dalit Literature and African American Literature

6.1 INTRODUCTION

Dalit literary criticism has included a comparative discussion of African American literature and Dalit literature. In comparing the two literatures, it has also been necessary to compare the African American and Dalit societies as well as their liberation movements. Since both societies are engaged in similar kinds of movements, examining them is an important component of the comparison of these two different communities and their literatures. Given that the two societies are different in terms of place and time, it is understandable that there should be certain limitations and differences in their literatures. On the other hand, there are similarities too. The characteristics of, and the similarities and contrasts between, the two literatures will have to be investigated, for such an endeavour can create a hospitable environment for the development of literature.

6.2 AFRICAN AMERICANS AND DALITS

Africans were captured, brought to America and sold since August 1619. This is when the slavery of African Americans begins. Dalit society, on the other hand, has experienced slavery since ancient times. Unlike the Blacks, whose motherland is Africa, from where they were captured to be sold in America, India is the motherland of the Dalits. They are not from somewhere outside.

The White settlers of America bought Blacks like cattle for farming purposes. In order to capture slaves, violent armed raids were carried out against African settlements. Those captured were gathered like animals. Some Africans also helped the White raiders. In order to teach the captured Black people a lesson, the White raiders subjected them to torture. The captives were beaten to death, or buried alive; they were hung by being nailed to the wall, or their ears were cut off and fed to them. Pregnant Black women suffered abortions from being assigned extremely difficult tasks. Black children, while still in their mothers' wombs were distributed as reward. Creditors became owners of unborn children upon non-payment of debts.

Slaves were always sold off for fear that they could rebel if their numbers increased. Children were separated from mothers, wives from husbands, and their families were destroyed. Whites constantly feared that if slaves lived together for too long, they would get too close to each other and rebel. Slaves ran away out of fear of being sold by their masters. There are hair-raising accounts of these tortures and excesses in Alex Haley's *Roots*.

For centuries, Dalits, branded untouchable, remained outcast. The Hindu varna system imposed slavery on them. They were tortured for a very long time. Such was the condition of the outcast communities that they had neither a village nor a home. Crime or begging was their only means of livelihood. The Adivasis lived in forests and caves.

God did not ordain the slavery of Dalits and African Americans. Human beings created it. Having imposed slavery on Blacks and Dalits, White and savarna societies forcibly extracted labour from them. Since the past and future of African Americans and Dalits always rested in the hands of their owners, their condition became extremely serious.

In 1706, the state of New York enacted a law to the effect that a Black's slavery would not end even after conversion to Christianity. Slaves could not give evidence against free citizens. There must have been a Manu somewhere in the minds of the Christians as well because Manu had legislated that the evidence of slave-Shudras against upper caste Hindus should not be accepted as proof.

Whites assigned separate educational institutions, separate eating places, separate spaces in trains and buses, and separate residential areas to African Americans. Untouchables, too, were kept outside the village. Arrangements were made for them to have separate settlements, separate river banks and separate cremation grounds. Since Shudras were denied any right to education by the Hindu caste system, the question of separate educational institutions did not arise. Later, during the British days, when they did begin to receive education, they had to sit in a separate corner or outside the threshold of the classroom. Actual descriptions of this arrangement can be found in P E Sonkamble's *Aathwaninche Pakshi* and Sharankumar Limbale's *Akkarmashi.*

6.3   SEPARATE BUT EQUAL

According to an order of the US government issued in 1863, all African Americans became free as of 1865. But in the 1896 case of Plessy versus Ferguson, the US Supreme Court propounded the concept of 'separate but equal'. According to this decision, it was not unjust to make separate but equal arrangements for African Americans in public life.

Dalits launched a movement to gain entry into the Kala Ram temple in Nasik. V D Savarkar then put forward a proposal to build a separate temple for Dalits. On 3 June 1927, Babasaheb Ambedkar expressed his opposition to this 'separate but equal' arrangement proposed by Savarkar:

> The idea of a separate temple is beautiful, but untouchability will not be eradicated if it comes into existence as a separate method for removing untouchability. Untouchables have to go to the temple, they have to assert their right like touchables. If untouchables could become touchables from separate arrangements, then untouchable Matang and Chamar separate

settlements have existed apart from times immemorial—yet what has been the result? (Ambedkar 1927b)

In 1954, the US Supreme Court judgement on Brown versus Board of Education of Topeka overturned the 1896 decision, declaring racial segregation to be unconstitutional. The law is a powerful weapon. It has been used extensively to protect African Americans and to obtain civic rights. The Dalit movement, too, has sought recourse to the law. The Mahad and Nasik agitations by Dalits were based on law.

Marcus Garvey said: 'Hold fast to the ideal of a dignified Negro race. Let us work together as one people, whether we are octoroons, quadroons, mulattoes or blacks, for the making of a nation of our own, for in that alone lies our racial salvation' (Garvey 1972a, 371). Babasaheb Ambedkar, too, has expounded at length on the issue of a common origin and identity in his *Who were the Shudras?* and *The Untouchables.*

African Americans since Garvey's generation have ridiculed the word 'Negro' and called themselves 'Blacks'. Similarly, Dalits have ridiculed the term 'Harijan' and named themselves 'Dalit'. African Americans changed their names in order to give up the names received from their masters, as those symbolized their slavery. Dalits, too, have abandoned the inauspicious and uncivilized names thrust upon them by the Hindu religion. African Americans underwent religious conversion with a view to end slavery. Dalits, too, converted due to their exasperation with untouchability.

If the Dalit is the protagonist of India's boycotted society, the African American is the protagonist of Black America. Both are slaves. The African American has been robbed and degraded by White society, and the Dalit by savarna society. The African American was bought and sold, and some of them paid their masters to buy their own freedom. However, in the Indian social system, freedom from untouchability cannot be bought, as it is imposed from birth. The African American slave could live in the master's house. White children could feed at a Black woman's breast. But even the touch and shadow of the Dalits were considered untouchable by the touchables. The irony here is worth noting: while the Blacks and Whites belong to different racial groups, the untouchables and savarnas do not.

The plight of African Americans and Dalits can be compared in a number of ways. While the African Americans were slaves, they could buy their freedom with money. Though Dalits were technically not slaves, they could not even pay to rent a house. The White master was responsible for looking after the Black slave. Since untouchables were not slaves, the savarnas had no concern for them. Untouchables are societal slaves. The cause of the African American's slavery was economic. The cause of the Dalit's untouchability is social. African Americans perform labour, but their labour is not considered undignified. Dalits do the lowest types of work, and their work is considered undignified. While African Americans cannot hide the colour of their skin, untouchables can hide their caste. African Americans were brought from Africa to America, Dalits belong to India.

There are similarities in the excesses and injustices committed against African Americans and Dalits, as well as in the sentiments of resistance expressed. The language and religion of wrongdoers may be different, but their source is the same. Similarly, though the nationality and religion of those against whom injustice is done are different, their pain is the same.

6.4 AFRICAN AMERICAN LITERATURE AND DALIT LITERATURE

African American and Dalit movements have proceeded along different paths and taken different turnings. But both movements are struggles for human rights and against exploitation. African Americans and Dalits experienced inhuman degradation; their struggle is against it. Despite differences of country, region, conditions, society and language, the similarity in the life experience of the two communities derives from the fact that both were targets of excess, injustice and slavery—their experience of pain is of a world-scale. There are similarities in the feelings of ownership, entitlement and superiority demonstrated by White and savarna societies, on the one hand, and of revolt against slavery by African Americans and Dalits, on the other. Because of these similarities, Dalit writers see the pain of African American writers as their own. African Americans have expressed their sorrow and pain through blues, ballads, stories, novels, dances and songs. Dalit writers have also communicated their pain through literature.

6.4.1 First Expression

The first expressions of African American and Dalit literatures were spiritual in form. The spiritual creations of African Americans were born out of their prayers for mercy. Such a desire for mercy is also present in the abhang of Dalit sants. The tone of early African American literature – expressing pain and arousing feelings of pity – is perceptible in the early phase of Dalit literature.

During its initial phase, African American literature took the form of folk literature. Many biblical subjects appeared in it. Black folk poets brought out works in their own dialects. Humour and pathos are expressed in these creations. The creations of African American folk poets are playful, predominantly entertaining, and popular. The beginning phase of Dalit literature is replete with poetry, folk theatre and folk art. Dalit folk theatre is meant for popular entertainment. Due to the Ambedkar movement, the face of folk theatre changed, and it was transformed into Ambedkarite jalsas.

6.4.2 From *Uncle Tom's Cabin* to World War I

The literary preferences of Black Americans changed during the period from the publication of *Uncle Tom's Cabin* (1852) to World War I (1914).

Harriet Beecher Stowe's *Uncle Tom's Cabin* gained instant fame. Written by a White woman, the novel threw heart-rending light on the life of African Americans. In the first year alone, 3,00,000 copies of the novel were sold—a very high figure for the 1850s. The book was translated into many languages and many organizations dramatized *Uncle Tom's Cabin*. Its many opponents also wrote anti-*Uncle Tom* books.

In 1901, Booker T Washington's *Up From Slavery* was published. Because of this book, Washington was regarded as the spokesperson for the Black community. But his writing expressed a respectful attitude towards the White society. By contrast, W E B DuBois's *The Souls of Black Folk* (1903), adopted a rebellious stance towards White society. Written in the same period, Washington's book reflects an appeal to tradition, while DuBois's work expresses a revolutionary consciousness against tradition. It is clear from this that despite similarities of time and cause, differences in writing arise due to personality and consciousness. Besides these two trends, African American writers engaged in *bellettristic* writing as well.

6.4.3   The New Black

World War I and its results brought about a fundamental shift in African American perceptions. Thousands of Blacks migrated from the south to the north, where they gained entry into various industries. They also entered the professions of education and politics, which increased their social support. A new consciousness emerged in the personality of the traditional Black person. Compared to the African American of the past, this was a new person. This transformation had an impact on Whites too. Besides, differences arose among Blacks and Whites vis-à-vis questions of descent. These differences were not only confined to Blacks and Whites; there were also inter-generational differences among the African Americans themselves.

Harlem in New York city became the centre of power for African Americans. In 1920, with the beginning of the Harlem Renaissance movement, it became the intellectual, economic and cultural centre for African Americans. The new Black person began to be formed here.

The period from the end of World War I to the beginning of the Depression era in 1929, was a time of hedonism and amnesia. Yet, this period also engendered feelings of helplessness and lack of enthusiasm. From 1920 to 1930, Claude McKay (1889–1948), Jean Toomer (1894–1967), Arna Wendell Bontemps (1902–1973), Countee Cullen (1903–1946), Langston Hughes (1902–1967), Zora Neale Hurston (1891–1960), Rudolph Fisher (1897–1934), and Wallace Thurman (1902–1934) did the major writing. During this period, African Americans came across as proud, fearless and highly energized. Their music, dance, art, painting and literature convey these sentiments.

African American writers have written about the experiences in their lives courageously, unhesitatingly and openly. These writers have not been concerned about White people. They expressed, with conviction and clarity, what seemed right to them. Langston Hughes's *The Weary Blues* (1926) and Jean Toomer's *Cane* (1923) may be mentioned as examples. Both writers undertook a campaign of rebellion in their writing, illuminated by a rebellious and proud self-consciousness.

After 1930, Richard Wright (1908–1960), Margaret Walker (1915–) and Ralph Ellison (1914–1994) inspired African American writers. Communist ideology began to surface in the writings of post-1930 writers. Richard Wright's *Native Son* (1940) is permeated with this ideology. Claude McKay went to the USSR in 1923, and his writing too espoused communist thought, though perhaps without the same force. George Schuyler, on the other hand, opposed communist thought. The African American poetry of this period is highly realistic and expresses the social problems facing Black people.

After 1940, realistic portrayal and a tone of defiance became stronger in Black writing. The years between the Depression and the end of World War II in 1945, were filled with helplessness, suffering and pain. The end of the war, instead of bringing peace, saw the beginnings of conflicts. The US had to confront many problems, internally and internationally. The arms race and the cold war with the USSR also had their impact. Besides, by the time of the Vietnam war, dissatisfaction among the youth and social unrest due to urban decline had also reached their peak in the US. This period was consumed by unrest, instability and fear of insecurity.

World War II was fought in defence of democratic values. Because of this war, declarations were made in support of freedom from want and fear, and freedom of speech and worship. But disappointment was the lot of African Americans. This, too, made a difference in Black consciousness.

In the post–World War II period, a heightened sense of resistance could be felt among African Americans. The Supreme Court decision of 1954 against racial segregation, Martin Luther King's civil rights movement of the 1960s, the non-violent boycott of buses in Montgomery, the Kennedy assassination of 1960, the coming together of thousands of Blacks and Whites in the same year to demand jobs and civil rights, and the enactment from time to time of legislation by the US Congress—all these led to the growth of intellectual unity and organization among African Americans. In 1966, a combative organization of their youth, called Black Panthers, came into existence.

The social and cultural make-up of African Americans changed in the period from the publication of *Uncle Tom's Cabin* to the emergence of the Black Panthers. Literature, society and agitation moved from a soft approach to a hard approach. Today's Black youth are completely different from Uncle Tom. They are Black Panthers, celebrating Black identity and Black consciousness: 'I am Black. Black is beautiful.'

In 1920, Babasaheb Ambedkar launched a weekly called *Mook Nayak*. The beginning of Ambedkarite consciousness can be traced to this event. This was also the period of the Harlem Renaissance movement. A good deal of the Dalit literature published during this time was consciousness-raising and propagandist. The works of Baburao Bagul, Namdeo Dhasal and Raja Dhale are examples of this trend in Dalit literature. The difference between these works and the writings of Bandhu Madhava, Shankarrao Kharat, Annabhai Sathe and N R Shende, as well as the *bellettristic* writing of the poet Grace is striking. And just as a White writer wrote *Uncle Tom's Cabin*, a novel on the life of African Americans, similarly, S M Mate, a savarna writer, published *Upakshitanche Antarang* (1941), on Dalit life.

The flame of revolution in the person of Babasaheb Ambedkar lit up and spread into the lives of the boycotted society, humiliated by an inequitable social system sanctioned by Hindu religion, and living a life of slavery. A community that had been living in the darkness of ignorance, clinging to the bottom rung of the caste-ladder, overturned the ladder. Compared to the traditional Dalit, this new Dalit of Ambedkar's movement is radically different.

Following India's independence, there were heightened political expectations in Indian society and in the hearts of the people. People's lives changed with the five-year plans, the elections, the decentralization of power, the public welfare schemes and the spread of education. With the introduction of a democratic system of government, common people began to understand the language of entitlements and rights. There was awakening at the lowest level, and hope that with independence all problems would be resolved. However, over time many of the problems got worse. Due to unemployment, poverty, increasing population, communal riots, corruption, communalization of politics, the din of Hindutva forces, excess and famine, Dalits lost faith in independence. In order to find solutions for their questions, the Dalit youth of Maharashtra launched their own organization, the Dalit Panthers, in 1972.

The heartfelt sorrow of Dalit life was narrated by Shankarrao Kharat in stories like 'Rama Mahar', 'Saangawa', 'Daundi', 'Aaba', 'Ramoshi' and 'Bhat'. But the Dalit to be found in these stories is quite different from the activist of the Dalit Panther organization.

6.5 BLACK CRITICISM AND DALIT CRITICISM

The societies and literatures of African Americans and Dalits bear considerable resemblance because the emotional worlds they inhabit – constituting their pain, rebellion, hopes and desires – are similar. Hence similarities can also be found in the criticisms of African American and Dalit literatures.

6.5.1   Objections to the Writings of White and Savarna Writers

White writers have portrayed Blacks in their literature. However, their portrayal has been distorted and full of contradictions. African Americans have been shown either as vile-natured and dirty, or as clowns. They have been represented in such a way that their inner core would appears as black as their skin colour. A realistic and accurate representation of African Americans cannot to be found in the American literature up to the Civil War. Marathi writers have not portrayed Dalits accurately either. Middle-class writers wrote novels about the lives of Dalits, based on their own imagination. Due to the absence of the authentic experience of Dalit life, these works are lifeless, shallow and distorted. Written from a middle-class liberal perspective, they fail to bring out the extreme self-consciousness and fighting instinct of Dalits. Both African American and Dalit critics have made the same objection: 'The portrayal of us bears no resemblance to us. The picture that you have drawn of us is repulsive and distorted. You do not have the capability to create a sharp and combative image of us.' That the White writers' portrayal of Blacks is inaccurate, is not the only complaint of African American critics. They have also objected to the representation of Blacks by certain African American writers. They have ridiculed works like Robert Hayden's poetry collection, *Selected Poems* (1966), James Baldwin's short story collection, *Going to Meet the Man* (1965), and John A Williams's travelogue, *This is My Country Too* (1965), for not expressing a strong Black consciousness. There have been similar criticisms of the writings of Shankarrao Kharat, N R Shende and Annabhai Sathe. Though savarna writers have been criticized for their failure to portray Dalits accurately, criticism of Dalit writers is an important development, for it shows that such criticism is not restricted by one-sided considerations of caste or race.

6.5.2   Who can Write Dalit and Black Literatures?

Prahlad Chendwankar has said: 'I have acute experiences of the

world and the life that I have seen. This is why I write'
(Chendwankar 1976). The African American poet, Gwendolyn
Brooks, has expressed a similar reaction: 'I write about people
and about circumstances that have been influenced by horrible
happenings in our society' (Freibert and Young 1989, 52).
Chendwankar and Brooks have identified similar contexts for
their writing. Whether they are African American writers or
Dalit writers, they convey their sorrow, pain and dissatisfaction
through their writing. Dalit writers' caste and Black writers'
colour shape their distinct experience. Colour consciousness is
the new experience of African American writers. This
consciousness is expressed in opinions such as, 'Our dialogue is
anti-racist'; 'Let those who truly love America join the valiant
Negro revolt, and change and save our country'; or 'We are the
most visible Americans'.

Dalit and African American writers hold that their experience
inspires them to write. This implies that other writers cannot
express their experiences. It is difficult to accept that non-Dalit
writers will be able to communicate the Dalit experience with
the same intensity as Dalit writers. With regard to Black and
White writers, Claude McKay's opinion must be considered: 'I
knew the chances for a black writer and a white writer were not
equal, even if both were of the same caliber' (McKay 1970, 316).
He believes that African American writers articulate their
experience with greater intensity, and this is why, later on, Blacks
made fun of *Uncle Tom's Cabin* by Mrs Stowe, a White writer.

There has not been a one-sided discussion which insists that
non-Dalits cannot write Dalit literature. M N Wankhede says:
'If non-Dalits have a broader experience, they too can write Dalit
literature' (Wankhede 1981, 60–61). In other words, Dalit
critics have recognized the possibility that non-Dalits could also
write Dalit literature. With respect to White writers, Alain Locke
says: 'Negroes could appreciate a white man's contributions to
the literature of their life if it were written in truth and beauty'
(Redding 1976, 45). White and savarna writers must portray
Dalits and Blacks in truth and beauty. Dalit and Black writers,
too, must depict their societies from a feeling of truth and beauty.

6.5.3 Opposition to Obscenity

Dalit and African American writers have opposed the writing of non-Dalit and White writers because their literatures have presented distorted and ridiculous pictures of Dalit and Black societies. But it is not only these writers who have engaged in unrealistic representations. Critics have also discussed the fact that African American and Dalit writers, too, have engaged in unrealistic and exaggerated writing. With respect to Dalit literature, Vijay Sonwane says:

> The Dalit narrative is inclined less towards ideas and more towards extended descriptions of sex. As a result, fundamental ideas have been de-emphasized, and distorted descriptions given greater weight. Readers with a prurient taste get great pleasure from this. Spicy renderings of sex are written and read with great interest. (Sonwane 1979, 21)

Dalit autobiographies like *Balut, Akkarmashi* and *Malaa Udhwast Whaychain* have also been accused of obscenity and sensationalism, and severely criticized.

The view that Dalit and African American writers give exaggerated descriptions of their societies for popularity, money and prestige, is heard in criticisms of both literatures. Addison Gayle Jr.'s comment on African American literature is noteworthy:

> It would be simplistic, even fatuous, to suggest that sole culpability for the distortion of black life through the 'propaganda of the word,' is attributable to whites in America and abroad. It would be fatuous, simplistic—and untrue. Those who have waged warfare against black people through the medium of words have often been black artists and writers themselves. The 'black exploitation' films and black television shows, peopled by brainless, untalented blacks, have presented images of black life as distorted, insulting and degrading as those presented by the American propagandists from Thomas Jefferson to Norman Mailer. Nor is the black writer immune to such criticism. (Gayle 1976, 38)

Dalit and African American literatures have been accused of obscenity. Criticizing Daya Pawar's *Balut* (1978), Vilas Rashinkar has written: 'Many aspects of sexuality are seen in many ways in *Balut*. The patience that he has shown in depicting this promiscuous life without reservation, is quite extraordinary. He has portrayed even mother, father, uncle and aunt in a repulsive manner.' (Pawar 1987, 23) Claude McKay's *Home to Harlem* (1928) too has been similarly criticized. Referring to the reaction of a black journalist, a member of what he refers to as 'the Harlem elite', McKay says:

> The journalist was a bitter critic of *Home to Harlem*, declaring it was obscene. I have often wondered if it is possible to establish a really intelligent standard to determine obscenity— a standard by which one could actually measure the obscene act and define the obscene thought. (McKay 1970, 315)

McKay has rejected the charge of obscenity leveled against him. Daya Pawar also condemns the accusation against *Balut*: 'The shame of the Dalits' past which seems repulsive should, instead of being felt by Dalits, in a true sense be felt by those who have imposed this disgusting life' (Pawar 1987, 16–17).

African American and Dalit writers have responded to the criticisms leveled against them. Neither has ever supported obscenity. These writers believe that people must understand the shameful and inhuman life that was imposed on Dalit and Black peoples. Objective reality cannot be ignored because it may bring a bad name to society.

6.5.4 Can Literature be 'Dalit' or 'Black'?

Marathi literature has developed through many literary traditions. Sant literature is still popular. All sant writing from ancient to contemporary times is called 'sant literature'—an identification that has never been questioned. Yet, with respect to Dalit writing, it is constantly asked whether this literature is 'just' Dalit. Literature is not Dalit, but it can be of Dalits. Though the caste system is the product of an established religious order that continues to maintain a stratified social system and nurture hierarchical ideas, yet it is expected that Dalit literature should not say this. How can such a demand be made? Discrimination among people is the product of established inequitable social systems. Literature has given voice to the consequences of this discrimination. As Gwendolyn Brooks has said about African American literature:

> Sometimes there is a quarrel. 'Can poetry be "black"? Isn't all poetry just POETRY?' The fact that a poet is black means that his life, his history and the histories of his ancestors have been different from the histories of Chinese and Japanese poets, Eskimo poets, Indian poets, Irish poets … The poetry from black poets is black poetry. Inside it are different nuances AND outrightnesses. (Brooks 1969, 12–13)

Because of their lower status in the social order, and the many cultural issues raised from serving the master society, there is a split in the mindset of African Americans and Dalits. It is certainly different from that of Whites and savarnas. Because of this different mindset and the inferior treatment received in every sphere of life, the emotional world and hopes and desires of African Americans and Dalits are distinct from those of Whites and savarnas. Literatures that reveal a universe and an emotional world dissimilar to those inhabited by Whites and savarnas have to be identified differently. The 'differentness' of these literatures is a mirror image of the writers' social and cultural distance. It is entirely inappropriate to ignore the social inferiority of Dalits and African Americans, and ask why their literatures are separate from those of the dominant society.

6.5.5   Approval of Revolt

Dalit and African American literatures are mirror images of the lives, sorrow and poverty of Dalits and African Americans. These literatures have been created through the chemistry of life and experience, society and problems, pain and rebellion. There are numerous expressions of red-hot experience and fighting instinct in these literatures. Dalit and African American literary commentators have rejected both the patronizing, sympathetic representations of White and savarna writers, as well as the unrealistic and pitying portrayals by African American and Dalit writers.

Commentaries on Dalit and African American literatures have approved of revolt. Yashwant Manohar says that 'Revolt is the most valuable truth in life and literature' (Manohar 1988, 21). He believes that revolt has creative energy. It destroys distortion and fosters culture. Regarding Don Lee's poetry, Brooks remarks: 'always, in the center of acid, beauties that are not eaten away!' (Brooks 1969, 12). African Americans and Dalits have embraced revolt. Stokely Carmichael and Charles Hamilton eloquently articulate the position of African Americans in their book, *Black Power* (1967). 'Our basic need is to reclaim our history and our identity from what must be called cultural terrorism, from the degradation of self-justifying white guilt. We shall have to struggle for the right to create our own terms through which to define ourselves and our relationship to the society and to have these terms recognized. This is the first necessity of a free people, and the first right that any oppressor must suspend' (Gayle 1976, 38).

Dalit and African American literary criticisms view literature as a form of movement for social liberation. Therefore, these literatures are discussed as vehicles for revolution, change, consciousness-raising, struggle and social commitment. The Black Arts movement subscribed to the ideas of Black Power, and opposed the efforts to alienate Black people from their society. This movement resulted from the cultural needs of the African American society. 'We are advocates of a cultural revolution in arts and ideas'—this was the proposal of this movement. It's conception of aesthetics was motivated by the intent to destroy White ideas and White world views.

Dalit literature is the literary movement of the Dalits. Concerning the need for this literature, Yashwant Manohar says: 'Establishing democratic socialism and determining the purpose of literature consistent with this is precisely the rationale for

Dalit literature' (Manohar 1978, 39). Similarly, Namdeo Dhasal observes: 'The liberation struggle of Dalits demands a total revolution. We do not want partial change; we need complete revolutionary change' (Dhasal 1973, 78).

Dalit and African American writers and critics consider their literatures to be weapons in the freedom movement. This is why revolt receives primacy in these literatures.

6.5.6 Acceptance of Humanism

Though the struggle of African Americans is against the injustices done to them, they support all oppositions to injustice. It appears that Dalits, too, take the side of all those who are exploited and oppressed, even though their fight is against the injustices being done to them. Dalits and African Americans speak and write about people who suffer from injustice in their own societies as well as in other societies. This is why the human being has become the centrepoint of both these literatures, and ideas of humanism have received approval in the commentaries on both literatures. Dalit and African American writers and critics perform a humanistic role, as the following statements demonstrate:

- Wheresoever the cause of humanity stands in need of assistance, there you will find the Negro ever ready to serve. (Garvey 1972b, 363)
- Black poets do not subscribe to death. When choice is possible, they choose to die only in defense of life, in defense and in honor of life. (Brooks 1969, 12)
- The world is becoming more and more to my liking, to my taste and in my image. It gladdens my heart to see black and brown men and women walk with dignity in the United Nations, in affirmation of the manhood and the self-hood of the entire human race. (Killens 1972, 612)
- Dalit literature is precisely that literature which accepts the liberation of humanity, regards the greatness of the human being, and strongly opposes the superiority of race, varna and caste. (Bagul 1980, 259)

Both Dalit and African American literatures raise their voice against exploitation. Their criticisms have primarily articulated ideas of humanism.

6.5.7 Need for a Sociological Perspective

The inferior status accorded to Dalits and African Americans in the established order, and the questions raised from living this inferiority, cannot be ignored when assessing these literatures. In order to appreciate the experiences of the separate settlements of African Americans and Dalits, it is necessary to study the established social systems. Without understanding the exploitation of African Americans and Dalits caused by inequitable systems, it will be difficult to comprehend the true meaning of the pain and rebellion articulated in these literatures. Therefore, the criticism of African American and Dalit literatures needs to be sociological. Prabhakar Mande's opinion on Dalit literature is worth noting:

> The event of the development of Dalit literature is not just a literary event. Therefore, this literature should not be viewed only from a literary perspective. Unless this literary chain of events is seen from a sociological perspective against the entire background of the changes happening in society, its significance will not be grasped. (Mande 1979, 66)

Mande's view is important. The necessity of using a sociological perspective in the criticism of Dalit literature should be kept in mind because the birth of this literature is social in nature. In this context, it is useful to note the comments made by Wole Soyinka, the Nigerian writer and critic, while discussing 'what constitutes, primarily, a critic's function'. He says 'attention must also be paid to the sociological conditioning of critics and criticism as a means of providing safeguards against an alien orientation of judgement or evaluation—a factor of which the critic may remain blissfully unaware' (Soyinka 1976, 2).

The importance of comparing the social context of Dalit and Black literatures becomes clear from the comments of Mande and Soyinka. It is essential to use a sociological perspective in the assessment and criticism of literatures whose very souls are constituted by 'society' and 'social problems'. A proper assessment or criticism of African American and Dalit literatures is not possible if society and social problems are set aside.

6.5.8 Readers of Dalit and African American Literatures

The Dalit's caste and the African American's colour—both of these are sources of never-ending pain. It is not as though established order has deemed only the Dalit and the African American persons to be hateful, it has judged even their emotions and feelings, hopes and desires to be repulsive. Members of the master society have never liked the language of freedom, equality, justice and self-respect spoken by slaves. Therefore, it has been suggested that White and savarna readers cannot like African American and Dalit literatures. An African American journalist told Claude McKay, 'the white reading public would not read good Negro books because of race prejudice' (McKay 1970, 316). Just as White readers could not know the sentiments of Blacks because of inherited bias, similarly caste-proud savarna readers could not understand the feelings of Dalits. As Daya Pawar says: 'Our entire society is not on the same cultural level. Due to the mentality formed by different cultural categories, caste system and customs in society, social life and world-views were divided. Because of the pressure of false morality, even the process of tasting a literary creation did not remain uncontaminated' (Pawar 1987, 8).

Claude McKay and Daya Pawar complain that White and savarna readers read their literatures with a prejudiced and contaminated mentality. This is a half-truth, because it cannot be denied that African American and Dalit literatures have received unprecedented welcome from some White and savarna readers. Describing the glory of Dalit literature, Pandharinath Ranade says: 'The flag of that glory which humanistic literary values had before the national struggle is again flying in Marathi literature because of the social and political pressure of Dalit literature' (Ranade 1991). On the contribution of African Americans to various forms of artistic expression, Redding says: 'Negroes were proud because something they had created was accepted as an expression of the national culture, was accepted as American' (Redding 1976, 44). These comments suggest that in White and savarna societies, there certainly are readers who wholeheartedly welcome African American and Dalit literatures.

6.6 OPPOSITION TO COMPARISON WITH AFRICAN AMERICAN LITERATURE

There has been opposition to the comparison of African American and Dalit literatures. Gangadhar Pantawane believes that the two literatures cannot be compared. Speaking at a seminar on Dalit literature in Kirti College, Mumbai, on 6 February 1977, he said: 'African American literature is referred to in the context of Dalit literature. But Blacks are not untouchable. Untouchability is a denial of humanity. This makes a big difference between these two literatures.' To be sure, Blacks are not untouchable, but they occupy an inferior place in White society. Like Dalits, they, too, have been assigned a 'place' on the hierarchical ladder. African Americans are mistreated because they are Black. They were assigned separate ghettoes. They rode in the back of the bus and ate in separate dining establishments. They could not move freely in their master's house. African Americans may well not be untouchable, but it must be acknowledged that their pain is as severe as that caused by untouchability. It is fallacious to say that Blacks have not been denied their humanity. The root cause for the endless acts of violence done against African Americans, and the damage that these have caused to human beings, lies in the denial of Black people's humanity.

Dalit literature placed before itself the ideals of African American literature. As a result, this foreign influence gained a stronghold on Dalit literature. This is the criticism of Bhausaheb Adsul. To him, this inspiration is 'un-Indian'. Mahatma Phule dedicated his book, *Gulamgiri*, to Black people. Does this mean that Phule's inspiration was un-Indian? But while some critics have opposed the comparison of Dalit literature with African American literature, others have welcomed it. Tarachandra Khandekar does not consider such a comparison un-Indian: 'It is essential to relate the inspiration of Dalit literature to that of African American literature. There is a commonality in the inspirations underlying developing and progressive societies' (Khandekar 1981, 68).

The comparison of these two literatures leads to the following conclusions. Firstly, African American and Dalit writers are searching for self-identity. Secondly, the experiences narrated in both literatures are based on inequality, and have been drawn from social life. Thirdly, insofar as African American and Dalit writers write out of social commitment, both literatures are life-affirming. Fourthly, the language of both literatures is the language of cultural revolution. And finally, there is a search for new cultural values in both literatures.

The opposition to comparisons between the two literatures has actually been very weak, and unsustainable in the face of argument. It cannot be denied that this comparison has created a nurturing environment for the development of Dalit literature.

6.7 CONCLUSION

African American and Dalit societies and their literatures are very much alike. The reason for this resemblance is that the emotional worlds of the two societies are similar. There are commonalities in their pain, their rebellion, their hopes and desires. Though their languages are different, the state of mind and the emotions expressed through these literatures are parallel. Besides, the histories of these societies, literatures and movements share a common direction. For these reasons, similar questions have been discussed in the criticisms of these literatures. Both Dalit and African American literary criticisms embrace revolt and humanism, and oppose obscenity, unnaturality and exaggeration. They view their literatures as movements for human liberation.

7

Dalit Literature and Aesthetics

7.1 INTRODUCTION

Savarna critics assert that Dalit literature should be critiqued strictly as literature. They assert that it is totally inappropriate to treat this literature from a reverential or sympathetic perspective simply because it has been created by Dalits. According to them, the literary evaluation of this literature should be based on literary criteria. They say that this may well be Dalit literature, but the reader will read it only as literature. Therefore, extra-literary considerations will have to be disregarded in its appraisal. But Dalit writers reject this point of view. It is their opinion that a middle-class criticism cannot properly evaluate this literature.

7.2 MARATHI CRITICISM AND DALIT CRITICISM

Savarna critics do not consider Dalit literature to be a separate stream. Besides this, or along with it, other literary streams with their own characteristics have also appeared in Marathi. Alongside Dalit literature, people from many other strata, engaged in different professions, have begun to write. Literatures have emerged from Dalits, villagers, Adivasis, Muslims, Christians, Jains, etc. In addition to contemporary literature, discussions have taken place about other literary forms as well, including science, workers', children's and feminist literatures. Literary circles in Vidarbha, southern Maharashtra, Mumbai, Konkan, Goa, Andhra Pradesh, Karnataka and Madhya Pradesh have worked for the development of literature. The discussion of Dalit literature has been influential in all these developments. However, from sants to Shudras, Marathi criticism has used the same criteria to judge and test all literary expressions.

7.2.1 Opposition to the Monopoly of Dalit Writers

In 1967, a seminar on Dalit literature was organized at Mahabaleshwar as part of the regional literature conference of the Maharashtra Sahitya Parishad. Along with Dalit writers, non-Dalit speakers such as Bhimrao Kulkarni, V D Ghate, Vidyadhar Pundalik and Kavi Anil participated in this seminar. While putting forward his position, Kavi Anil said: 'Literature written with a sympathetic perspective on Dalit life is Dalit literature.' At first glance, this point of view seems magnanimous. But behind this, a second view is invisibly at work. Kavi Anil does not accept that only Dalits will write Dalit literature. His position is that non-Dalits can also write Dalit literature, that it is not the monopoly of Dalit writers.

Vidyadhar Pundalik expressed the view that the belief – only Dalits can grasp the sorrow of Dalits – is true in a limited sense: 'It is possible to express the experience of Dalits with the power of imagination.' But Mr Pundalik does not make it clear as to where the imaginative power of non-Dalit luminaries has been hiding until now. Removing and cutting dead animals—how will non-Dalits write about this experience of Dalits with the power of their imagination? How will they feel the anger rising in the hearts of untouchables on the basis of their helpless imagination? Vidyadhar Pundalik himself does not want to come outside the boundary of the village, but the force of his imaginative power does! Is this not something? To answer Pundalik in his own terms, the ability of savarnas to express Dalit consciousness on the basis of their imaginative power is true only in a limited sense.

Other critics too have debated on who can write Dalit literature. Nirmalkumar Phadkule and Narhar Kurundkar hold that 'A savarna can also create Dalit literature. For this, it is not necessary that the writer should have been born as untouchable, because the basis of Dalit literature does not lie in one's birth in a particular caste. It is in social consciousness' (Phadkule 1986, 37; Kurundkar 1981, 96–97). Narhar Kurundkar shares Phadke's opinion that the basis of Dalit literature is the caste system that prevails here and the inspirational force behind this literature is the suffocation of enduring slavery from birth to death—therefore, 'non-Dalit writers can create Dalit literature'. However, this view is not acceptable to M S Patil: 'Being Dalit is significant, because it gives a distinct shape to consciousness' (Patil 1981, 3).

Dalit literature is that literature, which is written by one who is Dalit by birth, which is filled with rebellion and rejection, and which gives expression to Dalit consciousness. It is not possible to convey imaginatively the caste-specific experience of Dalits. Today, savarna critics think along two lines on this issue: 1. A non-Dalit writer can write Dalit literature with the power of imagination. 2. Only a Dalit writer can write Dalit literature. Between these two, the latter argument seems more realistic. The first is essentially based on imagination.

7.3 CRITICISM OF DALIT LITERATURE BY SAVARNA CRITICS

Dalit writers believe that Dalit literature is a movement. They see their literature as a vehicle for their pain, sorrow, questions and problems. But when readers read the works of Dalit writers exclusively as 'literature', the common ground between the writer and the reader is disturbed.

Dalit literature is life-affirming literature. All the strands of this literature are tied to life. It is the clear assumption of the Dalit writer that: 'My literature is my life, and I write for humanity.' How then can there be a purely aesthetic criticism of this literature? It needs to be decided whether the criticism of an artistic creation should be consistent with the writer's perspective or the critic's. When the writer and the critic view literature from the same perspective, there will be no fundamental inconsistency between a literature and its criticism. But when perspectives are different, the note of inconsistency will inevitably increase.

When the literature of Dalit writers is regarded as an artistic creation, the question arises whether conventional artistic values and literary criteria are sufficient.

7.3.1 Artistic Standards

'When measuring the significance of any artistic creation, only artistic values should be employed, all others are irrelevant—they are meaningless. If they were to have a place, it would be minor' (Rege 1968, 29). In other words, according to P S Rege, art should be considered only·as art. Dalit literature, being 'Dalit', cannot demand separate artistic yardsticks. It will have to be evaluated according to the autonomous and independent standards of art. To demand a different aesthetic for Dalit literature is like attempting to create a separate province—there is no justification for Dalit writers to develop a separate criticism. If their literature is great, it will stand any test, any time. Artistic values are not destroyed because they have been rejected. And, according to Balkrishna Kawthekar, if these values are rejected, Dalit literature will be deprived of a framework for evaluation (Kawthekar 1981, 12).

Kawthekar insists that Dalit literature must be assessed on the basis of traditional critical theories. There are universal values embedded in literature, which never change. This contention raises certain questions: How is Dalit literature to be critiqued based on these universal values? What are these universal values? Who determines them? What are these literary yardsticks? How were these developed? Did they originate in India, or were they imported from western literature? Do these literary standards change with time? Do they remain universal eternally? If they do change, when, and under what circumstances? Have critics prepared some mould or measure of these yardsticks for literary evaluation?

Such questions cannot be answered with the words: 'Universal values cannot be refused.' Dalit writers find these literary criteria obsolete. They believe that traditional Marathi aesthetics, which is based primarily on Sanskrit or English literary theories, cannot do justice to Dalit literature.

The act of imagination called art is impermanent and ever-changing. Literature changes with changing culture. Unless the yardsticks change, the relationship between literature and criticism will be fractured. In India, there are tremendous differences in levels and processes of taste. What is tasteful to one person may not appear so to another. In these circumstances, it will be wrong to insist on fixed standards. Like literature, criticism, too, is apt to change. Just as the course of literature has changed from one period to another, so has the mode of criticism. To assert that someone's writing will be called literature only when 'our' literary standards can be imposed on it is a sign of cultural dictatorship. The yardsticks of literature do not remain standstill for all time. With changing times, literature changes, and there remains the possibility of change in its criticism too. New literary trends cannot be evaluated with traditional literary yardsticks.

Thus, two trends can be identified in the criticism of Dalit literature: 1. Dalit literature should be evaluated on the basis of universal literary values. 2. Literary standards do not remain fixed for all time, therefore, the criticism of Dalit literature cannot be based on traditional measures. Dalit critics are in agreement with the latter, because they have broken with traditional middle-class values. M N Wankhede holds that 'Dalit writers should abhor values determined by middle class writers and critics' (Wankhede 1981, 77).

Even if there was something fixed or definite about the criteria for evaluating uses of the imagination, a mechanistic approached must be avoided. Otherwise, the practice of criticism will be impeded. Critics use different approaches. This is the natural process of criticism; it is never of one kind or form. Criticism has to analyze and discriminate between artistic creations and point out deficiencies. More than one set of yardsticks should be used in evaluating an artistic creation. For the proper assessment of the many dimensions of a work of art, exceptional commonality between artist and critic, and a multi-faceted way of thinking are necessary. It would be inappropriate to insist on fixed yardsticks, if there is to be a proper evaluation.

7.4 THE NATURE OF CRITICISM OF DALIT LITERATURE BY SAVARNA CRITICS

Savarna criticism of Dalit literature differs in nature from Dalit criticism. G M Kulkarni asks: 'Isn't it miraculous that four to six volumes should have been produced rapidly on Dalit literature, which came and gathered momentum after rural literature, and not a single book taking the pulse of rural literature should exist?' (Kulkarni 1984, 9). The implication of this question is obvious. Kulkarni regrets that there has been no criticism of rural literature, though it has existed since 1925. Sadly, he complains how Dalit literature, which developed later, suddenly gathered such momentum that so many works of criticism came out in short order. In fact, he seems displeased in having to acknowledge this prolific discussion of Dalit literature.

According to V L Kulkarni, even if the narrative in a Dalit text appears ordinary, it still has the undoubted capacity to convey pain to the readers (Kulkarni 1998, 56–58). If 'giving extraordinary pleasure' is considered an artistic value, why cannot 'giving extraordinary pain' too be recognized as an artistic value? Being technically ordinary or artistic has to do with craft. Is artistic technique more important than meaning in a work of art? When an artistic creation definitely disturbs, even though it is 'artless', either its lack of artifice will become a minor issue, or it will have to be acknowledged that this quality of 'artlessness' is, in fact, its literary value.

N S Phadke has propounded that novels cannot be written based on incidents in the lives of untouchables: 'The kinds of contexts and events that are needed to add colour to a novel are not found in Dalits' lives' (Phadke, 152). The firm and solid foundation on which the majestic structure of the novel stands is not to be encountered in untouchable life. Phadke finds it difficult to build this structure from the hut of the untouchable, but Arun Sadhu, Jaywant Dalvi and Madhu Mangesh Karnik have written novels on Dalit life. Dalit writers have published numerous novels. Because of his formalistic perspective, Phadke cannot see events and contexts in the lives of Dalits as worthy of gripping fiction.

In Kusumavati Deshpande's opinion, it is difficult for Dalits to find an articulate voice and be technically skilled because they are deprived of all sanskara (Deshpande 1987, 3). This implies that all sanskara-equipped non-Dalits possess an articulate voice and technical skill. But this is not the ground reality. Further, when non-Dalits inflict such torture on Dalits, how can it be said that they are cultured? It is a sign of their middle-class mentality that Phadke cannot find impressive contexts and events in Dalit life, and Deshpande cannot see culture in it. At the Maharashtra Sahitya Parishad seminar on Dalit literature in Mahabaleshwar, Bhimrao Kulkarni posited that: 'the irritation and anger of Dalits are false, while their complaints are twisted and ridiculous.' In order to forestall any misconception that may result from his view, it is necessary to refer to what Babasaheb Ambedkar had said, evidently anticipating just such an accusation:

> The allegation against us is that our policy is one of aggression. We do not make our demands humbly. As a result, people who are disposed in favour of removing untouchability, turn against us. But it seems to me that those who make this objection should feel shame, if not publicly, at least in their minds. Who else in this whole world is as courteous and helpless as the untouchable? Have we not been courteous for hundreds of years? Please do not teach us lessons in courtesy and humility now. It is not as if we are habitually arrogant, or we like to indulge in discourteous attacks. Whether we will find food for our stomachs even after a day's hardship, this worry is our daily companion. Humanity is superior to food. Since even the simplest rights of humanity do not escape your clutches, we have to struggle. (Ambedkar 1928b)

Balkrishna Kawthekar suggests that Dalit writers need to go beyond rejection, rebellion and revenge, and see people as people (Kawthekar 1981, 16–17). Does this mean that the Dalit writer does not view people as people? Does Kawthekar not know that the ordinary, exploited person is the focal point of Dalit literature? He expects Dalits to regard all human beings as people, because, when this happens, questions of rejection, rebellion and revenge would no longer arise. But, among human beings, there are some who are exploiters and others who are exploited. The very justification for Dalit literature lies in siding with the exploited and taking a stance of rejection, rebellion and revenge against exploiters. If to Bhimrao Kulkarni the irritation and anger of Dalit literature seem false, to Balkrishna Kawthekar its sentiments of rejection, rebellion and revenge appear anti-people. In sum, the rebelliousness of Dalits is not to the liking of savarna critics such as Kulkarni and Kawthekar.

7.5 LIMITATIONS OF THE CRITICISM OF DALIT LITERATURE BY SAVARNA CRITICS

Non-Dalits have critiqued Dalit literature from its early days. In a display of their magnanimity, they have guided Dalit writers. Many people are ready to dispense advice and provide direction. In fact, there are more non-Dalit critics than Dalit critics. Critical commentaries on Dalit literature have been published in the form of books as well as articles, speeches, interviews and forewords. Some non-Dalit critics have praised Dalit literature, while some others have condemned it. Non-Dalit critics are divided into two groups—supporters and opponents; there have been friendly as well as negative criticisms.

7.5.1 Adulatory Criticism

Non-Dalit critics have praised Dalit literature out of a feeling of intimacy. They have encouraged and worshipped Dalit writers, and have put forth ideas to guide them. The writing of such non-Dalit critics resembles the pretence of a patron. It provides superficial support, but it neither provokes thought nor does it inspire.

7.5.2 Negative Criticism

It is not as if non-Dalit critics have only supported Dalit literature, they have also criticized it. Further, they have reacted negatively to the various proposals for Dalit literature. Dalit writers have been criticized for writing as well as for not writing. For example, it has been alleged that a Dalit writer's output ends after writing one autobiographical book. It has also been suggested that since autobiographical writing does not require scholarship and talent, the Dalit writer can write nothing else. It has been said, too, that Dalit literature is shallow because of lack of artistic sophistication. Questions have been raised, as well, to the effect that since Dalits are pilferers, thieves and criminals, how can they be regarded as exploited?

These are some of the ways in which there has been negative criticism and inappropriate praise for Dalit literature. Even now, many literary critics overlook the burning inspiration present in it and constantly harp on its shortcomings. While this carping is certainly bad, even more misleading would be to pat Dalit writers on the back like a guardian. Both the positive criticism that flatters Dalit literature and the negative criticism that is characterized by prejudice, will prove equally fatal. Dalit literature would be able to perform its historic task well, if it were to be evaluated with a balanced and welcoming attitude, and an objective perspective.

7.5.3 True Criticism has not Occurred

Although non-Dalit critics have done a great deal of criticism of Dalit literature, Dalit writers remain dissatisfied. Their complaint is that a proper criticism of their literature has not happened. Many of these writers have commented on the incompleteness of Dalit criticism by non-Dalit critics. During a personal discussion at the Second Mandesh Literature Conference, Sangola, Maharashtra, on 12–13 November 1991, Waman Howal observed: 'My story was analyzed, but it does not end with the ending. There, too, I have to say something. But no one gets to that point.' Dadasaheb More, in conversation at Nasik on 11 February 1992, said: 'What is the meaning of Dalit criticism? Critics only give opinions on incident and context. What kind of criticism is this?' Daya Pawar, in a personal discussion that took place during the

65th All India Marathi Sahitya Sammelan at Kolhapur on 31 January 1991, said:

> Critics neither understand the description of social context in Dalit literature, nor fully grasp the meaning of language. They do not know idioms and phrases. Nor does anyone read in depth. No one ever makes the effort to understand. Critics don't even seem to realize that we live in a different cultural island. They pay no attention to the distinction between a literature written from imagination and one that is based on lived ideas.

Uttam Bandhu Tupe contends: 'Critics destroyed my autobiographical book on Matang society' (Tupe 1983, 162). Finally, Datta Bhagat, in a personal discussion on 7 January 1997, remarked: 'Criticism of Dalit literature began to be written alongside the creation of Dalit literature. This is why the criticism has been so imprecise. New commentators presented their criticisms after reading the existing criticism. In fact, criticism should be done after reading the literature.'

The complaint that the criticism of non-Dalit critics is not accurate and truthful is understandable. But we must also reflect on how many Dalit writers have written on Dalit literature. Dalit writers only write forewords to the books of emerging writers. They speak in literary conferences and seminars. They like to present their views as conference presidents and guests. However, they do not write about the work of other Dalit writers. When a new work by a Dalit writer appears, it is received in silence. In the meantime, non-Dalit critics discuss and critique Dalit literature. The fact is that the discussion of Dalit literature survives because of the writings of non-Dalit critics. Established Dalit writers do not write on the works of new Dalit writers. This narrowness on their part should also be taken into account. In this context, Gangadhar Pantawane's books, *Vidrohache Paani Petale Aahe* (1976), and *Vadal che Vansaj*, are significant.[1]

---

1. Translator's note: Dr Gangadhar Pantawane, educationist, critic, (*contd.*)

On the one hand, there is the narrow focus of the Dalit writers, and, on the other, are the shortcomings in the assessments by non-Dalit critics. Dalit criticism is stuck within these boundaries. Because these boundaries have not been broken, savarna criticism suffers from its own limitations. For example, a considerable proportion of savarna critiques of Dalit literature suffers from shallowness. Also, there is a distinct tendency to expose the instances of one-sided, monotonous and sub-standard writing and publishing found in Dalit literature. There is also an attempt in savarna critiques to sever the Dalit writers' links with tradition and culture. And, finally, there is a total absence of sociological literary yardsticks. All these limitations point to the need for a Dalit literary criticism.

7.6 AESTHETICS OF DALIT LITERATURE

The discussion of the aesthetics of Dalit literature received an impetus from Sharad Patil's *Abrahmani Sahityanche Saundaryashastra*. He made us aware that since Dalit literature did not have its own aesthetics, it had to rely on Brahmanical aesthetics: 'It must be considered why counter-revolutionary literature possesses the weapon of aesthetics, but revolutionary literature does not' (Patil 1988, 6).

Patil refers to aesthetics as a weapon, and believes that revolutionary literature must acquire this weapon. Because he has described middle-class, upper-caste literature as Brahmanical or counter-revolutionary, should it, therefore, be conceded that the aesthetics of Marathi literature is like a weapon? How does it

(*contd.*) mentor of many Dalit writers, is respected as the 'elder statesman' of Maharashtra's Dalit literature movement. He was principal of Milind College, Aurangabad, founded by Dr Ambedkar. It is at this college that the early discussions of the need, form and purpose of Dalit literature took place. In 1967, Dr Pantawane launched the literary journal, *Asmita* later called *Asmitadarsha*, which has played a critical role in the development of Dalit literature. He is the author of numerous works of critical appraisals of Dalit writers.

matter anyway? Has Marathi literary aesthetics not been used already as a weapon against Dalit literature? It is necessary to explore these questions.

7.6.1   Aesthetics of Marathi Literature

The idea of beauty has been discussed in the criticism of Marathi literature. B C Mardhekar, R V Patankar, Surendra Barlinge, Narhar Kurundkar, M P Rege, Sharatchandra Muktibodh, D V Kulkarni and Prabhakar Padhya have made important contributions to the literature on aesthetics.

7.6.1.1   *'Pleasure' as Aesthetic Value*

Rather than being concerned with the form of an object, the concept of beauty tends to revolve around the feelings of pleasure and empathy aroused by viewing the object. The pleasure and empathy generated by beauty concerns aesthetes. Artists have to tailor the beauty of their work in a way that is agreeable to the tastes of aesthetes. The preferences of aesthetes are important for the artist. Aestheticism believes that the impact of a work of art on the audience must be pleasure born of beauty.

Everyone has a sense of beauty, but only the aesthete has the aptitude for tasting beauty. The ability to imagine beauty is the gift of high culture. In N G Chapekar's opinion, 'To experience beauty, a cultured mind, health and enthusiasm are necessary' (Chapekar, 66).

The aesthete is a product of circumstances. But in the processes of taste, the aesthete is as important as the artist and the artistic creation. And this is why one must recognize that beauty-related experiences are object-specific, person-specific and situation-specific—there cannot be a general concept of beauty. However, the aesthetics of Marathi literature has given primacy to the pleasure of the aesthete.

7.6.1.2   *Aesthetics and Dalit Literature*

If pleasure is the basis of the aesthetics of Marathi savarna literature, pain or suffering is the basis of the aesthetics of Dalit literature. Will readers be distressed or angered, or will they be pleased by reading the pain and revolt expressed in Dalit literature? It is a literature that is intended to make readers restless or angry. How can the aestheticism in discussions of beauty be reconciled with the 'Dalit consciousness' in Dalit literature? This revolutionary consciousness is based on ideas of equality, liberty, justice and solidarity, rather than pleasure. This is why it is important for Dalit critics to change the imaginary of beauty. In every age, the imaginary of beauty is linked to prevailing ideas. At one time, for example, kings and emperors used to be the subjects of literature. But today, the life lived in huts and cottages situated outside the boundary of the village has become the subject of literature. It has become necessary to transform the imaginary of beauty because it is not possible to investigate the creation of Dalit literature and its commitment to revolt and rejection within the framework of traditional aesthetics.

Dalit literature is a new literary stream of the post-independence period. Not only is it new, its form and purpose too are different from those of savarna Marathi literature. Therefore, it cannot be appraised using traditional aesthetics.

7.6.1.3 Rasa Theory and Dalit Literature

Yadunath Thatte has proposed that, with Acharya Jawdekar having recognized 'revolt' as the tenth rasa, 'cry' should be accepted as the eleventh rasa (Thatte 1990, 9). However, what would be the advantage in increasing the number of rasas? Essentially, would this not be simply tantamount to proving the incompleteness of the prevailing rasa theory? According to Madhav Aachwal: 'Which 'rasa' is this—only after tasting, slowly sipping, and with every sip, relishing its taste, feel, smell, as the "tastiness" spreads in the mouth, can this be known' (Aachwal 1972, 7). Could Dalit literature be tasted in the way described by Aachwal? The answer would have to be in the negative. How will the taste of the pain, anger, rejection, rebellion, problems, struggles, injustices and ill treatment contained in Dalit literature be known through slow sipping and relishing? In terms of Dalit literature, the rasa theory of aesthetic appreciation seems insufficient. This is why Yadunath Thatte has demanded an increase in the number of rasas. But there has not been a widespread discussion of the feasibility of extending the rasa theory to Dalit literature. A few articles have been written about it, but critics of Dalit literature have not taken notice of these.

7.6.2   Position of Dalit Writers on the Aesthetics of Dalit Literature

Dalit literature is not pleasure-giving literature. Consequently, the aesthetics of Dalit literature cannot be based on the principles of an aestheticist literature that privileges pleasure derived from beauty. This is why there is a felt need for a separate Dalit aesthetics. Since the need for a separate aesthetics for Dalit literature has been demonstrated, does it mean that what is or is not beautiful in Dalit literature will also have to be proved? Would it be necessary to determine which subjects are beautiful and for what attributes?

7.6.2.1 *Materialist Aesthetics of Dalit Literature*

In formulating the aesthetics of Dalit literature, it will be necessary, first of all, to explicate beauty. Is such an explication possible? It is not possible to do so on the basis of imagination and conventions. The traditional theory of beauty seems abstruse and spiritualistic. According to this theory, the beauty of an artistic creation lies in its expression of world consciousness or other-worldliness. This traditional theory is universalistic and spiritualistic. The aesthetics, which proposes that the beauty of a work of art is its artistic rendering of reality, is materialist. Dalit literature rejects spiritualism and abstraction, its aesthetics is materialist rather than spiritualist.

7.6.2.2 *Aesthetics of Dalit Literature and Ambedkarism*

Ambedkar's thought is the inspiration for Dalit writers. While critics certify that the artistic creations of some Dalit writers are up to standard, they label others sub-standard. If all Dalit writers who create these supposedly standard and sub-standard literary works share the same source of inspiration, why is there a qualitative difference among them? The answer will lead us to the source of an aesthetic for Dalit literature.

All Dalit writers are inspired by revolutionary Ambedkarite thought, and articulate life-affirming values in all their literary creations. However, Dalit literary works cannot be accepted as beautiful for these reasons alone. The standard of a work of literature depends on how much and in what way an artist's ideas – embedded in the work – affect the reader. Dalit writers will have to decide how best to express Ambedkarite thought in their literature. That work of Dalit literature will be recognized as beautiful, and, therefore 'good', which causes the greatest awakening of Dalit consciousness in the reader.

First of all, Dalit writers will have to become one with their inspiration. They will need to acquire a heightened consciousness of literature in order to give literary expression to their inspiration and their experience of it. The deeper the relationship of readers with a Dalit writer's inspiration, the greater will be their liking for the work. The artist, the artistic creation, and the reader—all three are important components of this process. The artist's personality is reflected in the work, and the reader's personality is unified with this reflection. The artist and the reader become one in the artistic creation. This meeting of the two depends on their possessing common values. The intensity with which Dalit readers will feel the Dalit writers' experience, will not be shared by non-Dalit readers. On the other hand, there will also be a difference in the degree to which non-Dalit and Dalit readers will find the Dalit writers' experience unique, because the experience is a part of the Dalit readers' daily life. It should also be kept in mind that while the concept of beauty in Dalit literature cannot be a universal concept, the Ambedkarite inspiration expressed in it can be of universal value.

7.6.2.3 *Dalit Literature and the Question of Preference*

Aestheticist criticism examines how a work of art influences the mind and heart of the reader. The artist, the creation and the aesthete form the basis of this criticism. In it, primacy is given to the aesthete's response. Evaluation and taste hold an important place in the review of any literature. Without these, criticism remains incomplete. When matters of evaluation and taste are raised, it becomes indispensable to discuss the issue of the reader's preference. In this context, a number of propositions can be formulated: The reader is an important participant. This reader's preference is already or yet to be formed. The reader has certain pre-determined assumptions that precede reading. The reader examines whether these assumptions are challenged or confirmed by the text. The same work is liked by one reader, and disliked by another. The reader's mindset is informed by class and caste. The reader's capital is his or her prior reading.

This consideration of the reader's preference is crucial. And along with the reader and the creation, the artist also plays an important role, the work of art being the artist's creation.

Dalit literature cannot be fully appraised without knowledge of the Dalit writers' experience, their anger, rejection and rebellion vis-à-vis traditional values, as well as the social context. Any disjuncture between the experiences found in an unfamiliar literary text and those in the critic's life becomes an obstacle in the process of enjoyment. Enjoyment of literature is related to proximity, and that depends on the mind and heart of the connoisseur. The art that entertains the connoisseur does not cause problems of preference. But the art that contradicts tradition obstructs the process of enjoyment by casting a shadow on the conscious and unconscious prejudices and assumptions held by the reader.

Dalit writers give priority to problems of society over the entertainment of readers. They express their feelings in their literature. They do not create literature with urbane readers in mind. Their effort is to transport the aesthete-readers to their own level of experience. Because Dalit writers are not focused on the aesthete-reader, traditional aesthetic values, which *are* aesthete-reader centred, are not applicable to the evaluation of their literary productions.

7.6.2.4 *Freedom as Aesthetic Value*

Are human beings only beauty-mad? Do they only want pleasure? The answer to both questions is no, because hundreds of thousands of people appear to be passionate about freedom, love, justice and equality. They have sacrificed themselves for these ideals. This implies that for them social values are at least as dear to their lives as, if not dearer than, values of art. Equality, freedom, justice and love are the basic sentiments of people and society. They are many times more important than pleasure and beauty.

There has never been a revolution in the world for the sake of pleasure and beauty. Many governments have been overturned for equality, freedom and justice. This is history. The literature that glorifies pleasure gives central place to the pleasure-seeking aesthete. The literature that promotes equality, freedom and justice is revolutionary, and it emphasizes the centrality of the human being and society. If pleasure-giving literature arouses joy and sympathy in people, revolutionary literature awakens consciousness of self-respect. This difference must be heeded in the context of P S Rege's remark on revolutionary literature: 'It is not possible for literature to be larger than revolution' (Rege 1968, 22). The writings of Rousseau, Voltaire and Karl Marx caused revolutions. Because of the writings of Phule and Ambedkar, strong mass movements have emerged, and continue to emerge. Rege's dictum does not apply to every kind of literature.

The literature of the exploited is primarily concerned with the search for freedom, and giving expression to it. All aspects and dimensions of freedom are seen in it. We should remember that the imaginary or idea of freedom has an aesthetic aspect, as much as it has political, economic, social and moral facets. The sentiment of freedom is present in Dalit literature not only as its life essence, but also as beauty. The three values of life – equality, freedom and solidarity – can be regarded as constituting the essence of beauty in Dalit literature. The aesthetics of Dalit literature rests on: first, the artists' social commitment; second, the life-affirming values present in the artistic creation; and third, the ability to raise the reader's consciousness of fundamental values like equality, freedom, justice and fraternity.

Babasaheb Ambedkar's thoughts are the inspiration for Dalit literature, and Dalit consciousness underlies the creation of this literature. It is a consciousness against slavery. Values of equality, freedom, justice and solidarity are inherent to this literature. This Dalit consciousness motivated by Ambedkarite thought occupies a central place in the aesthetics of Dalit literature. If we examine why it is necessary for Dalit writers to write, the relationship of the artist to the work of art and the society is clarified. The description of the aesthetics of Dalit literature is hidden precisely in this consideration.

7.6.2.5 Standards of Dalit Literature

The following standards can be set down for the evaluation of Dalit literature.

- Artists must be motivated by their experience.
- Artists must socialize their experiences.
- Artists' experiences must have the strength to cross provincial boundaries.
- Artists' experiences must seem relevant to all time.

Although the aesthetics of Marathi literature developed by savarna Marathi critics privilege pleasure, it is not a weapon. The savarna critics have not been able to use such aesthetics in the context of Dalit literature.

7.7 CONCLUSION

Savarna Marathi critics have written voluminously on Dalit literature from its beginning. There are more savarna than Dalit critics of Dalit literature. Their critique of Dalit literature is mired in the issue of taste. It comprises of flattery, advice, direction and sympathetic encouragement. Dalit writers do not find this criticism genuine.

The savarna critics have engaged in favourable and unfavourable criticism. One group supports Dalit literature, and another opposes the unquestioning approval. The latter believes that Dalit literature should be appraised as literature and not be worshipped simply because it is written by Dalits. In its opinion, though savarna critics have insisted that the criticism of Dalit literature should draw on eternal values, it does not seem as if the critics have actually undertaken this kind of criticism.

Dalit writers have rejected traditional artistic standards and aesthetics, and have attempted to develop a separate aesthetics of their own. But there is no need to indulge in the theatrics of staking their entire intellectual prowess in proving the incompleteness and incompetence of traditional, established aesthetics. What is the point of asking for the name of the village to which one is not going? Our path is different. Our direction is different. Therefore we should spend our energies in traveling our own path and seeking our own direction.

8

Dalit Literature Today: A Conversation with Sharankumar Limbale

ALOK MUKHERJEE

On 9 and 10 March 2001, Sharankumar Limbale and I had a long and wide-ranging conversation on issues concerning the state, prospects and direction of Dalit literature. The conversation was held at his residence in Pune. I asked him several questions not only about his own work, but Dalit literature in general. Limbale was a gracious host, and he answered my questions willingly, readily and in detail.

AM: Will you tell me something about your new novel? You were telling me about its title, 'Upalya'. You were saying that it has to do with a tribe of monkeys. Where did it come from?

SL: After Babasaheb Ambedkar passed away in 1956, Dalit society no longer had a guardian. This huge vacuum required that, after him, Dalit society and movement should have a leader. The followers of Dr Ambedkar came together and decided to form a collective leadership to give shape to Babasaheb's dream of building the Republican Party of India as a political organization of Dalits. However, the collective leadership failed due to infighting. The party split into groups—one went with the Congress and the other remained Republican. People felt that the leaders were feathering their own nests, instead of dealing with the injustices. Babasaheb's dream remained unfulfilled. That is when a group of young people established Dalit Panthers. These Dalits, who were young students in 1956, completed their studies in the 1960s. They felt there was no one to lead Dalit society after Babasaheb. They took it upon themselves to create an organization to give society direction, and fight against social problems and the caste system. Taking inspiration from America's Black Panthers, they founded a revolutionary, militant organization called Dalit Panthers, on 9 July 1972. The Dalit Panthers led a huge movement. *Upalya* is about this movement. This novel narrates the Dalit movement that came into being after the death of Babasaheb Ambedkar. The novel is about a Dalit youth, who after completing his education, gets organized and engages in struggle, becomes an activist, and fights for social causes. The establishment attempts to buy such combative Dalit youth. Or else, it fabricates police cases, or even kills them in staged encounters.

The young Dalit Panthers started a movement to demand that Marathwada University be renamed after Babasaheb Ambedkar, because it is in this Marathwada region of Maharashtra that Babasaheb founded Milind College and initiated higher education for Dalits. He gave higher education in Marathwada a new direction; therefore, the university should be named after him. The Dalit Panthers launched a large-scale movement with this demand, and many of its activists came to the fore as militant leaders. The political establishment called upon them, invited them into the government, gave them the party ticket. It formed alliances with those who did not join the party, and took them into committees. Thus, those who had been militant leaders, were now involved in party politics.

AM: These people went into the Congress or …

SL: No, no. They joined the Republican Party, which is the Dalit party. And here, the man who was their hero, Ramdas Athawale, was made a minister. Athawale and I started our activist careers together. I continued to work with him when he became minister. I saw how a movement began, and how it came to an end. Sickened by this experience, I have written *Upalya*. This novel is a document of social and political happenings between 1956 to 1996.

About the term 'Upalya'—it is a tribe of monkeys in which the male monkey constantly dominates the female monkey, exploiting her. When another male monkey is born, he kills it so that it may not usurp his place. And he does not allow new males to be born. Our political system resembles 'Upalya'. Every leader wants to occupy the chair himself and·does not allow a rival to surface. He wants sycophants or courtiers, not other leaders. When a new generation comes up, and someone from it tries to become the leader, he is corrupted and then eliminated. This tendency can be termed 'Upalya', and that is the name I have given this novel.

AM: I haven't heard about this tribe of monkeys. Is the belief about such a tribe prevalent in this region or in Marathi folklore? Where did you come across it?

SL: I was not familiar with it either. I first came across this concept in an article that Dadasaheb Rupawate, a major leader of the Republican Party of India, wrote for a book I edited. In it, he wrote that the establishment of the Republican Party is the establishment of Upalyas. Ever since I heard it ten years ago, I wanted to use this word as the title of an artistic creation.

AM: I have read a portion of this novel. There is quite a bit in this segment about the role of writers in this revolutionary movement. It seems you are examining this question with a great deal of attention.

SL: Writers, of course, play a leading role. You will see that behind every revolution that has happened, writers have made major theoretical contributions. Whether it is the French Revolution or the Russian Revolution, or the freedom movement in India, literature has prepared the background. Among us, Babasaheb Ambedkarji has written as well as agitated. And so has Mahatma Phule. For us, it is not as if the writer and the activist are separate. It is the same person who is an activist as well as an artist, an activist as well as a poet. The Dalit Panther movement was a movement of writers. Other people – the common people – joined later. The role of writers was to ensure that the movement does not stray from the thoughts of Ambedkar and Phule. The role of the writers was to convey this consciousness to the people through literature.

AM: What, then, is the purpose of writing? You have said that the writer's job is to take literature to the masses. Surely, this has an impact on the kind of writing that happens. Then, there is the question of who are the masses that you are trying to reach? Is it only the Dalit society or others beyond it too?

SL: No, it is not as if the Dalit movement is exclusively for Dalit society. Dalit questions are linked to the caste system. Until the caste system is annihilated, our problems will not be eradicated. These questions will not be resolved only because Dalits have agitated, got organized in the early 1960s, and embraced transformative thought. The answer to these questions is in the hands and hearts of the whole savarna society. This will not be a matter of weapons. We do not believe in violence, we adhere to non-violence. Our war is a war of ideas. Dalit literature seeks to transform savarna society, to bring about change in the heart and mind of the savarna individual. Dalit literature will have two dimensions. One will be to familiarize Dalits with their past, to explain to them that they are enslaved, to show them that they are human beings and it is their duty and their right to fight for the rights of a human being. The other dimension of Dalit literature will involve working on the hearts and minds of savarna society in order to persuade them about the rights and entitlements of Dalits, to make them see that these are human beings and have been suppressed, and convince them that they must change.

AM: This, then, raises the question: is the same writing appropriate for both purposes?

SL: ·Yes, it is. When Dalit readers read my autobiography, *Akkarmashi*, which has been translated into several Indian languages, they write from all over India to praise me: 'You have confronted us with the degrading life that we have led. Yes, you have made us realize that we must get united to fight.' On the other hand, when savarna readers read this book, they write to me, 'Limbaleji, we feel ashamed that our ancestors have committed such excesses on your society. We feel that this is very shameful.' It is very good that such feelings and sentiments are produced in the savarna reader. It generates a guilty conscience in the savarna reader; and not only guilt, but also a conviction that the injustices and excesses that have been committed against Dalits must not continue. So, the same book can generate these different responses.

AM: If that is the purpose of your writing, how does it affect what you write? For instance, in *Upalya*, you are looking at the rise of a movement, what happened to it and how it came to an end. Middle-class writing is mostly concerned with a family or an individual. The texts deal with psychological issues, relationships, love, personal tragedy. What has been your subject matter? What kind of writing do you do?

SL: First, it is clearly my intention as a Dalit writer to set alight the feeling of self-respect in Dalits, to introduce them to the idea of self-respect. Second, I have to generate a feeling of humanity towards Dalits in savarna readers. Dalit writers should take up subjects that are consistent with these two objectives. Consequently, only those stories, novels, poems are part of Dalit literature that deal with the rights and entitlements of Dalits, and the progressive movements of Dalits. Detective fiction or lyric poetry, even if written by Dalit writers, cannot be Dalit literature. I, too, have done other kinds of writing, but no one recognizes them as part of Dalit literature. Only that literature written by Dalit writers can be called Dalit literature, which concerns Dalits, which is inspired by the Dalit movement, and which is conscious of the ideas of Phule and Ambedkar.

AM: So, are you saying that, for a work to be called Dalit literature, it is not sufficient that it be written by a Dalit writer?

SL: The subject matter of writing and the consciousness underlying it are of the utmost importance. Further, even when a Dalit writer is writing about a Dalit subject, the work cannot be called Dalit literature if it presents the subject in a cheap, popular way. It must contain Ambedkar's thought, the thought that teaches Dalits the feeling of self-respect, and the language of rights and entitlements.

AM: Do other Dalit writers accept the view you have expressed, or is there a debate?

SL: No, no. Every Dalit writer is influenced by this perspective. In every writer's book, in every writer's writing, there is bound to be a line such as 'My writing is inspired by the thoughts of Babasaheb Ambedkar.'

AM: Some time ago, I had read an article by Dr Dharmavir in which he had said that there is a need to go beyond what has been learnt from Babasaheb. He said that whatever Babasaheb said paved the way for us, but if we remain stuck in it, we will not be able to move forward. And as I recall – I read it a year ago – he said it is fine to keep on writing about Brahmanism, but we need to leave that behind and work for ourselves and our own progress.

SL: No. The view expressed by Dharmavir is symbolic of a middle-class mentality. Several people here in Maharashtra also express similar views. They say Babasaheb Ambedkar did not find another follower, another disciple. Phule had Babasaheb Ambedkar for a disciple, but Ambedkar did not find any and so his movement did not continue. It is false to believe in a single saviour or in divine incarnation. It is not that the path opened by Babasaheb Ambedkar must be taken forward. However, as long as this path remains, it will be Babasaheb's. As far as the sun's light goes, it belongs to the sun. That does not mean that someone must take it further. There is a kind of mentality that simply wants to criticize. Instead of criticizing, why does Dharmavir not offer some options himself?

AM: He says Dalits must give up this obsession with Brahmanism. Dalits should not worry about Brahmans, they should write about their own welfare, their well-being, themselves.

SL: In every movement there are all kinds of ideas. People think in many ways, but a view that deviates from the movement cannot be considered universal or as being commonly held. Only someone sitting in an ivory tower can say that Ambedkar's thought has been exhausted, that it needs to be questioned, now that we are moving towards globalization. For that matter, Buddha and Krishna and Mohammad and Christ are ages old. Surely, all of them had to be born at some point in time, and die at some other point in time! But their ideas never died. Ambedkar's thought is relevant for our times. It will remain valid as long as this caste system continues. It would have died if it had been the thought of an individual. Ambedkar's thought is the thought of every downtrodden person. As long as there is a caste system in this country, and there is inequality, this thought will continue to hold sway. And as it continues, there will be many different tendencies, many different views, and it will keep growing. Ambedkar's thought does not belong to some one individual named Ambedkar; it is the thought of those who are writing and publishing in the entire Dalit society. The fact that Dalit literature is being produced due to the influence of Ambedkar's thought simply means that every day collections of poetry, novels and works of criticism are being added to it, not being deleted from it. Down the road, other kinds of writing, other ways of thinking will develop. As time changes, this thought will evolve. It will not end.

AM: Recently in Delhi, I heard a lecture by Dr Namwar Singh. He was expressing his worry that identity politics, such as it exists in Dalit literature, will result in narrow boundaries at a time when, to fight globalization, a new form of internationalism is needed.

SL: What is the context in which people are talking about globalization? Whenever the issue of globalization comes up, people will talk about information technology, about the World Bank, about free trade. Is this globalization? No, this is a surface view, having to do with certain practices. We need to think about the major cultural globalization that is about to happen. The arrival of other cultures in India will cause a big upheaval in the orthodox thinking here. It will change the caste system. Our youth are running after other options—will this be good or bad? I say that this will be good, because there needs to be change. The water of this change will flush away the dirty sewage that is our society.

AM: So, you think cultural globalization can have a good impact?

SL: It can have a positive impact. It can change the Indian people. The entire belief system here needs to change. Because of globalization, we are becoming aware of democratic practices and of struggles for rights and entitlements from across the world. Today's women are different from yesterday's women. And the women of the future are going to be even more different. It is extremely important for this change in terms of rights, entitlements and freedom to occur.

AM: But there are arguments that globalization will reduce people's rights, entitlements and freedom.

SL: No, globalization is increasing, rather than decreasing people's rights and freedom. I feel that these people are saying the opposite because they are afraid that it will destroy Hindu culture. India must become a melting pot. Cultures of the whole world – of Germany, Japan, China, Russia and America – should come here. A world system should materialize, only then the caste system that has developed over thousands of years will change. One Babasaheb Ambedkar is not enough. This system has not changed even though we had Buddha and Mahavira. It has been changing slowly, but globalization has accelerated the speed of change. It needs to increase even further so that the old face of this society is transformed.

AM: I see a strange contradiction in that the same forces that are propagating Hindutva with such energy are also encouraging globalization through the government that they control. Why would they do this if, as you are saying, globalization can undermine Hindutva?

SL: They want to hold on to their Hindu vote bank. And the Hindu vote bank is gradually moving towards globalization due to a sense of practicality and realism. When the ancient belief system clashes against the reality that is coming in the wake of globalization, a new culture will emerge. We are not accepting western culture holus-bolus, we are giving it an Indian face. This has happened in the case of Dalit writers too. Dalit writers speak with great emotion about the village. They say that we experienced tremendous injustice and ill treatment in the village. And yet, even when Dalits leave the village and come to the city, and even when they change their names, they still remain connected to their village identity. For example, a Dalit from Sholapur will alter his old repulsive name to Sholapurkar! Every

Dalit, who has changed his name, has then adopted the name of his village. In other words, even here, you will see a contradiction. They are hitting at the old social system, and at the same time they maintain some relation with the system in which they have lived through some good and some bad moments. I see a love–hate relation in this. There is tremendous rebellion in our hearts against the Hindu social system. And yet, when this system comes under attack from the outside, we think about it with a little bit of affection. Such is our love–hate relation with Hindus.

AM: Will you then say that Kancha Ilaiah's negation of Hinduism in *Why I Am Not a Hindu* is an aspect of this love–hate relation?

SL: Yes, that is so. The whole struggle of the Dalit movement is based on the demand that the upper caste should accept us. But they are not ready to accept us, though their hearts are now changing a little. Babasaheb Ambedkar's first agitation was to assert that Dalits have the right to drink water from the same tank from which upper castes drank water. Animals drink water from the same tank as they do, birds drink from it too, and yet, Dalits cannot drink water from it, though they belong to the same religion as the upper castes. This is inequality. It is not as if we will become immortal by drinking the water of this tank, but we should be able to drink water. But it was not acceptable to savarnas, and this is why Babasaheb started the agitation. Second, Babasaheb agitated for entry in the Kala Ram temple. He claimed that if Shankaracharya could go to the Kala Ram temple, so also could an untouchable, because both are Hindus. The untouchable has the same rights with respect to god as Shankaracharya does. Why can Dalits not go to a temple into which a dog can enter, a bird can enter? It is not as though we will become immortal by going to that temple and by viewing the god, but we should be able to go to the same temple. This is a battle for equality. And if they had conceded Babasaheb's demand, he would not have spoken the language of conversion. In 1935, Babasaheb said, 'I was born a Hindu, but I shall not die a Hindu. I shall abandon Hindu religion.' He did right to embrace Buddhism, which was a form of rejection. The first course is to talk to them with love about the struggle for acceptance. And the second course is to leave them if they do not agree. Dalit struggle has moved along both these courses.

AM: Do you see any change since this struggle began?

SL: There has been a big change. I am now 45 years old. The social system today is very different from that which existed when I was a youth. There are roads now, there is electricity, there is television. But I am not talking about these changes. There is change in the hearts and minds of the ordinary savarna masses. They have begun to think about the rights and entitlements of Dalits, which they did not before. Dalits are now organized to fight for their rights. They have been given legal protection, and provisions have been created for them in the Constitution. The law is with them, the Dalit movement is with them, all progressive-minded people are with them. Therefore the savarnas are thinking about the rights and entitlements of Dalits. I think that this is the biggest achievement of the Dalit movement.

AM: What has been the effect of this change on Dalit literature?

SL: Dalits have created Dalit literature, to be sure, but it is the progressive savarnas who have promoted it. There was a time when savarna publishers and editors would not publish Dalit writing. But once Dalits started writing, founded their own publishing houses, brought out their own papers and magazines, and established an independent identity, they attracted the attention of savarnas. It is an unfortunate characteristic of India that the upper castes pay us no attention when we are a part of them. But when we come out of their fold, they do.

Dalit literature, too, has created its own distinct identity. The non-Dalit critic, the non-Dalit publisher and the non-Dalit reader have played a major role in creating this distinct identity, in enabling Dalit literature to emerge. Traditionally savarna literature is very imaginative, not realistic. The literature that readers got to read from the puranic age until the present, tended to be entirely imaginative or fantastic. The real face of the common person was absent. With the rise of Dalit literature, readers could witness Dalits' sorrow, they read about the Dalits' struggles for their rights, they encountered the real human being, a new human being. And everyone approved of this literature. Because of this approval by progressive savarnas, Dalit literature developed further. Instead, if they had rejected it, Dalit literature would not have grown the way it has.

AM: You are referring to the Dalit person. Is today's Dalit similar to the person of forty years ago? Has there been a change?

SL: There has been a big change. Forty years ago, Dalits were unable to struggle against the people of their village. They submitted to the existing social order. Today, even those Dalits who live in the villages are aware of the ongoing agitation and they fight for their issues. When faced with injustice, they come to their activists, their movement. There were injustices against them in the past, and there are injustices today as well. But when these happened in the past, they did not react. They did not have the spirit of resistance. Today, Dalits are conscious that injustices are being done to them, and that they should fight back. They are aware of their oppression.

AM: If you take the English collection, *Poisoned Bread*, edited by Dangleji, most of the stories and autobiographies in it are about village life. In most of the childhood memoirs, writers have shown how helpless they were. There was extreme ill treatment, but there was nothing to be done about it. This *Poisoned Bread* is taught even today. I myself have taught it at the university in Toronto. Will you say that the portrayal of Dalit life in the stories and memoirs in *Poisoned Bread* is no longer accurate, that it is of historical importance?

SL: No, that is not so. The change has come about in the minds and hearts of Dalits, not in the system. The village is still the same, the settlements surrounding the village, the bastis, remain as they were. Even today, Dalits have to struggle—for water, for survival. There are battles over every issue. Earlier, the battles used to be over the fact that they were untouchable. Today, the fights have taken on a political colour. Two rivals are facing each other. In the past, the village used to strike at an individual: 'This bastard is causing waves, if we cut him up the whole lot of them will be silenced.' But today, one individual is not destroyed, the whole settlement is burnt down, an entire community is murdered. This only means that, whereas previously, there used to be fire in the heart of one individual, today the heart of the whole community is aflame. Such is the battle between the savarna and the untouchable.

AM: What, then, has been the effect on writing?

SL: This is bound to affect writing. The generation that was writing forty years ago is now coming to an end. It is no longer writing. That generation's literature was concerned with past memories, past time, past history. Today's Dalit literature must think about the present times as well as the time to come. But Dalit writers do not think about the injustices taking place today; they still write about the past. Nor do they reflect on the tomorrow that is to come in their lifetime. This is because they do not know what is to come. For that, a visionary Dalit writer has to appear. Any ordinary person can produce the kind of writing that has been done concerning past history. It is very easy to write, 'I was born; I was assaulted by savarnas; I used to beg.' It is not as if there is a great deal of talent in this kind of writing, or that this is great literature. It is a different experience; this is why readers read it. But literature requires vision. And that vision should be such that it takes the common masses forward, and makes them aware of their condition in today's context. Unless this happens, I worry that Dalit literature may become stagnant.

AM: Why do you think so?

SL: It is because of the movement. Until now, Dalits were the subjects of every Dalit movement. And the leaders interpreted the issues on the basis of the past. Whenever leaders made speeches, they hurled abuses at *Manusmriti*. They criticized the system that existed at the time of bhagwan Ramchandra, or the age of the *Mahabharata*, or the period of the sants. Contemporary injustices and ill treatments were interpreted by reference to these examples. And it was said: 'Even today we are facing the injustices that were meted out to us thousands of years ago. When will these end?' But we would not have come to this if the unjust acts of today had been interpreted in terms of the movement of democratic ideas around the world. I am afraid that the views of our leaders and activists – their reading, their thinking – have been marked by narrowness of ideas. Whenever there is ill treatment against Dalits, they agitate. Whenever a Dalit is killed, they agitate. Whenever the eyes of a Dalit are pulled out, they agitate. Whenever a Dalit basti is boycotted, they agitate. But they do nothing when there is violence in Kashmir. They do not think when a man like Harshad Mehta engages in corruption. They are not affected by all that is happening in Punjab. Globalization is approaching. What will be its impact on our movement, our literature, our society? They do not think about it. How are we being left behind by the entire education system? How are we being cheated of the various employment opportunities and, indeed, by the whole establishment? They do not think about these. It seems to me that it is this parochial thinking that has brought about our current situation.

AM: Okay, but the question still arises: why this parochial thinking?

SL: Such thinking was much needed when I was a youth. Then, the appearance of a beautiful woman, even a fairy, did not distract me, because of the issues facing our society. Injustices were being done to Dalit women; our parents were being ground under by pain and sorrow. And that was the context in which we were thinking that all this suffering was being caused by Hindu religion, Hindu mythology and the puranic texts. We felt that this base must be destroyed. We must pollute the sacred Hindu texts, think and write and talk about them. Our need then was to pollute the sacred tradition that was thousands of years old, to critique it, and to insist that this was not our tradition. That was our need at that point, and that is what we did. But we also needed to envision the future, and it did not happen.

The second thing is that progressive-minded people, who made a large contribution to the Dalit movement, are no longer with the Dalit movement. They used to join every agitation initiated by the Dalit movement, and work on issues concerning Dalits, because there weren't too many Dalits working on these issues. But today, there are many Dalit activists and leaders working for Dalit concerns. Dalits are waging their own struggles. They no longer ask progressive people to work on Dalit issues because now Dalits have their own independent organizations. Progressive people, too, played a paternalistic role. They came to Dalits in the same way that Christian missionaries approached Adivasis. Instead of a missionary approach and mentality – that is, 'we have come to lift you up' – they ought to have said, 'We are coming with you; you are the leaders and we are your activists.' Instead, they came as leaders, and we had to be the workers. They gave speeches, and we listened. And they used to make speeches about what we were living through. Why were they telling us, when they needed to tell their own people? They should have created awareness in savarna society, and they didn't. So, the progressive-minded people did half a job. The upshot of this was when these people sided with Dalits, savarna society sidelined them, saying, 'They have gone over to the Dalit side, they are betraying us.' Now, the Dalit movement should have welcomed the people who, leaving behind their own society, had come to us. But they were looked upon with suspicion: 'They belong to the other side; they are not our people. How can they be our leaders? Why should they fight for our interests? Moreover, they do not even have the moral right to fight. We will be our own leaders.' Therefore, Dalits also boycotted them. Rejected by both sides, progressive savarnas lost badly. The reason for the defeat of progressive thought and the emergence of reactionary thought in the later decades of twentieth century is that while, on one hand, progressive-minded people did not raise awareness in savarna society, on the other, they were not accepted by Dalit society. As a result, revivalist forces have surfaced and the Dalit movement is on its own.

AM: I see new themes emerging in whatever Dalit literature I have read in Hindi. Earlier I referred to the kinds of subjects dealt with in *Poisoned Bread*. Now, for example, I see stories about what happens to a Dalit individual after he's completed his education, found a government job, and even become an officer. Not only what is happening to him in savarna society, but what is happening inside him, in a psychological sense. I've read several such stories. It seems to me that Dalit writers express a new concern now as to what price people are paying for progress.

SL: Yes, and the shape of Dalit literature is also changing. Dalit literature used to portray history; now it has started to deal with what is happening to the Dalit who has become an officer, what kind of love the young Dalit finds, etc. And, people have begun to write about the difference between yesterday's struggle and today's struggle. This is the beginning of change in Dalit literature.

AM: This new writing – I have only read it in Hindi – which is about the middle-class Dalit individual, to what extent does this writing fit your definition of Dalit literature?

SL: Dalit literature is not concerned only with the experiences of those who are left behind, oppressed and powerless. A Dalit can also be an IAS (Indian Administrative Service) officer. Recently, a higher level IAS officer has published his autobiography. We have called it a Dalit autobiography because whether you are a foot soldier here or an IAS officer, you have to struggle against the mindset of the caste system on a daily basis. A soldier's struggle can be different from an IAS officer's, but it is a struggle all the same. Here, a Dalit minister in the government has to fight the caste system. Even the former President of India, K R Narayanan, who is a Dalit, had to fight it. We ought to see the struggle against casteism – be it that of an ordinary citizen or the country's president – within the parameters of Dalit literature.

AM: In your writing, you have defined who a Dalit is.

SL: Quite so. The Dalit is untouchable. This is the correct definition, and the writing is meant for the untouchable. The untouchables are fighting, and the writing is raising consciousness about human rights among them. This is the limited context in which we are waging our movement. But it won't be good if the movement remained so limited. We must include the entire Bahujan society. Today, we must use a language that includes this wider community as participants in our struggle, as the audience of our writing, and as people whose awareness we are raising. Unless we find such a language, we will be left alone, the struggle will be splintered, and everyone will be distracted and defeated. Therefore, we need a language that speaks to all the dispossessed, wherever they may be, whichever country, whichever community. Whether they are savarna or White or non-White, if they are downtrodden and exploited, they are one of us. It is essential to propose this kind of thinking. Only then can it be decisive.

AM: This raises another question. Of late I have heard some people say, 'Well, this is Dalit literature and that is DNT (Denotified Tribes) literature. Laxman Gaikwad is a DNT writer; he is not a Dalit writer.' It seems that these people are making fine distinctions such as this. What do you think about it?

SL: No, no. Whether one is untouchable, DNT or Adivasi, we consider all of them to be Dalit. In Maharashtra, Laxman Gaikwad is recognized as a Dalit writer, and he says, 'I am a Dalit writer.' But it is the intellectual class that is making these distinctions for their own analysis and their research purposes. In Maharashtra, the DNT, the SC (Scheduled Castes) and the ST (Scheduled Tribes) are small groups. And they have joined together in the struggle. Only when you see each group on a nationwide basis, you realize that DNTs form a very large group, and so do the SCs. Distinctions between oppressed groups can be made for the purpose of study only in this wider sense. But their issues, their struggles and their sentiments are alike, and they have worked in concert. I think group identity should be distinguished from political action.

AM: You mentioned intellectuals. You may have read Mahasweta Devi's plays and stories. She writes only about Adivasis. As far as I know her work, she has not written on the other issues. It seems that some, savarna or non-Dalit, see the problem in very small units.

SL: That's fine. The issues should be seen and worked on in · small, discrete units. That is how this work can be done. For example, when we do a blood test, we take only a small quantity of blood for testing. We have such a large number of communities and tribes. It is absolutely not possible that one institution or individual can pay attention to all of them. It is important that Mahasweta Devi should work for Adivasis, Laxman Gaikwad should work for his community, and Sharankumar Limbale for his. But the common thread is that we have to work for those who are oppressed and left behind. Even though I am working for my community, my role and ideas are the same as those of people who are working alongside every other oppressed and deprived community. This is how we must think. We will go wrong if we looked upon a Sharankumar Limbale or a Mahasweta Devi in isolation.

AM: The other dimension of this question is this: if Dalit literature is the literature of the dispossessed, and the Dalit question is the question of the dispossessed, then what is the difference between this definition and Marxism's definition of the same issues? After all, Marxism also talks about the dispossessed.

SL: Of course, Marxism talks about the dispossessed. In India, Marxism came into the hands of the savarna people, the Brahmans. The struggle that they initiated was the struggle between the capitalist and the dispossessed. What is most regrettable about the Indian Marxists is that they made no effort to understand the caste system. They did not recognize that Marxism in the Indian context had to fight for the end of both the caste system and the feudal system. We began to fight in the context of the economic system. When there is an agitation or a strike in a mill here, Dalit as well as savarna workers are involved. All of them agitate, take part in the strike, and shut down the mill on economic issues related to wages and increments. But when these workers, who agitate together inside the mill, are outside the gate of the mill, they go to their separate caste colonies. When there are caste or communal riots, these very workers throw stones at each other's houses. Marxists organized the workers inside the mill, but they did not organize in the colonies where these workers went back to live. It is important that there should be a feeling of equality in the places where these workers live their lives. It is not enough to promote a feeling of equality only in relation to work-related struggles. Just as I am linking the Dalit question with the wider question of the dispossessed, similarly, Marxism, too, should have waged the battle for equality in both the mill and the colony. They only fought inside the gate of the mill, while the workers fought against each other outside.

AM: So, you are saying that there would not have been much of a difference between Marxism and what we are calling Ambedkarism, if Marxists had fought in the mill as well as the colony.

SL: None at all! Why should there be difference? Even today we do not consider Marxism to be the thought of an enemy. It is the thought of an ally, because it opposes inequality, as does Ambedkarism. And the thought of Black people against White racism, too, opposes inequality. Wherever it may be in the world, and whatever form it may take, every thought that expresses opposition to inequality is Ambedkarite thought. It is our thought. When the idea of opposing inequality emerges in our Dalit colony, it is called Ambedkarite thought. When it is expressed inside the mill, it is called Marxist thought. When it is applied to White racism, it is called the Black revolution. The labels may be different, but the idea is the same, that is, opposition to inequality. Anyone who is a slave, wherever in the world, is one of us, and we have to fight beside them. That is my role. This is the slogan of the Dalit writer and of Dalit literature.

AM: But within that, the caste system has its own particular role and it is very important to bring that into the open. Recently I was at a conference where people were talking about caste-based discrimination. But then some people began to talk about many different forms of inequality, and the discussion of casteism as a particular form of inequality disappeared. I have found that this does happen sometimes, and what is called specificity is lost.

SL: Yes, and precisely for this reason we have seen ourselves distinctly as Dalits. But this does not mean that those who are untouchable are not poor. Untouchables too have economic problems, and they can be resolved through Marxism. But economic issues are not of import to us in isolation. Along with those, we have issues of our self-respect, our fundamental rights, our status. 'We are human beings': This language, this idea, is of even greater importance to us than economic issues. We will talk about money and food later. Before anything else, we are human beings—we will first talk about this. This is because we have not yet been recognized as human beings, our voice is deemed untouchable, our shadow is treated as untouchable, our touch is considered untouchable. Our colonies have been kept apart. We are expected to wear dirty garments, and use dirty language. Our culture is regarded as dirty. We are required to assume dirty names. Our first task was to erase this condition. We are on fire; we will first extinguish it. Then we will see how we shall eat. Yes. We are burning, and still we will eat. This cannot be. We cannot even fall in love. How many love poems are there in Dalit literature? Almost none. Why has this happened? It has happened precisely because young people, angry young people, have written Dalit literature. Don't they feel sexual attraction? Do they not have feelings of love? Of course they do. But compared to sexual attraction and love, they found their rights, their status, and their respect to be more important. And they wrote about these. Only now, after a whole generation of writing, they are coming to these subjects. Love poetry is now being produced. People have begun to write about sex. And as these trends develop, the full form of Dalit literature will become clear.

AM: I see that you have put together a collection of Dalit poetry. When were the poems in it written?

SL: They are old, from two decades ago. And the Dalit love poems in it are different from the love poetry of middle-class writers. The love poetry that Dalit writers write is quite distinct.

AM: Tell me something about it.

SL: In this poetry, the beloved, who is a Dalit woman, is an activist. She works alongside her lover. She is prepared to die. Her face is not like the moon, and her cheeks are not heavenly. She is an ordinary woman, and her love is ordinary. She is a labourer, a worker, and whenever there is a struggle, she is the giver of strength. That is the figure of the beloved in this poetry. The other lover is the one who loves a Dalit, but when she discovers his caste, she abandons him. This is the savarna lover. Dalit youth have found two kinds of love. The first kind is the love they found from women in their community. It was true love, based on a relationship of equality. The other was the love they found in savarna women. When this woman gets to know her lover's caste, she says, 'No, sorry, you are an untouchable. I am leaving.' The love poetry that involves Dalit women is forward-looking. There is no separation in it, no breakdown of relationship. But the love poetry about savarna women is marked by breakdown, it expresses bitter feelings towards savarna women.

AM: Have women also written love poetry?

SL: Yes, women too have written, and the lover in their poetry too is seen as an activist on an equal footing. Dalit love poetry does not present the beloved and the lover as sex dolls. We are two soldiers in a battle, a movement. We are two activists; we have to fight together. It is not the love poetry in which they go to the garden or stroll by the sea. 'Come, you organize and I am with you. We have to take the struggle forward. We have to finish the battle.' They come together not to chit-chat. When they talk, they talk about the injustice and oppression taking place in society.

AM: I have seen that Dalit literature is often compared with Black American literature. Where did this interest in Black literature come from? And why only in Black literature of the United States?

SL: When we got to read about the mistreatment of African Americans by White Americans, it seemed to us that it was very similar to the mistreatment of untouchables by the savarna society here. And we saw a great resemblance between the pain and the ill treatment of the two. This is why we do not consider African Americas to be strangers; we see them as one of us. Their literature seemed to us to be our literature. We felt that we should write just like them against savarna society. When? The idea came to those who were writing at the beginning of the Dalit literary movement. Today Dalit literature has evolved considerably, and we are no longer concerned with Black literature. We know how we should write and what we should write.

Earlier, when no one was writing, there was a discussion, and I shall say something about it. In those days, students of Milind College used to write poetry, which was put up on the noticeboard. Those boys were writing love poetry. They were also publishing love poetry in a magazine published by the college. M N Wankhede, who taught at Milind College, had gone to America for his PhD, and had read Black literature there. He said to the boys in Milind College hostel: 'What are you doing? This is wrong. In America too there are people like us who are writing poetry, bringing out magazines and other publications, staging dramas. We should emulate them.' Professor Wankhede started a Dalit literary magazine, *Asmita*. He organized a two-day discussion, which was the first discussion of Dalit literature. Several intellectuals were invited to discuss the shape of the Dalit literature that was to come. During that discussion, a couple of scholars said that it should be revolutionary literature, a literature that takes us forward, a literature like that of America's Black people. Then people started discussing what constituted this progressive or revolutionary literature.

Janardhan Waghmare began to publish numerous articles in *Asmitadarsh*, a Dalit magazine started by Dr Gangadhar Pantawane, based in Aurangabad. Later, he collected and published them in *Black Identity*. Dalit writers were introduced to Black American literature due to Waghmare's articles. No one had read Black literature in the original, but they were influenced by the discussion that was taking place. I myself have not read this literature. I am such a big writer of Dalit literature, even I have not read it! For one thing, it is hard to find. And even when it is available, it is in English. Our Dalit writers here do not know much English, and, moreover, they do not fully understand the cultural references. We read whatever becomes available in Marathi, and that tends to be in the form of articles and essays. Subsequently, when Dalit literature began to be published extensively, people began to do research on Black writing, write articles on it, and make comparisons. Dalit writers themselves were writing about the experiences of their communities. They were expressing the anger towards the established social order. They were neither concerned with what was happening in America nor worried about how they should write. They were expressing themselves. But it is the critics here, the elite class, the intellectuals, who were comparing the two.

AM: I find it an interesting question, and also a puzzling one. As you said, Dalits should be connected to the dispossessed globally. There are many other oppressed people in the world, I find it curious as to why there was such an interest in African American literature and not in any other.

SL: One reason is that the Black people there are victims of social injustice. They were mistreated because they were Black; their being Black is the reason for their mistreatment. And that is why they were enslaved. White people were not enslaved because they were White. I find a tremendous similarity in their being Black and our being untouchable. If they had not been Black, I do not think we would have felt this closeness.

AM: There is one very odd thing. Richard Wright was a major African American writer. His two works, *Native Son* and *Black Boy*, are very powerful. He was a member of the Communist Party of USA, because of which, during the McCarthyism of the 1950s, he and the famous Black actor and singer, Paul Robeson, had to leave America and live in Europe. When the Bandung Conference of the non-alignment movement was held in Indonesia, that brought together Nehru and Indonesia's Sukarno, China's Zhou Enlai, Yugoslavia's Marshal Tito, Egypt's Nasser, etc. Richard Wright attended it and wrote a book on the conference. He was very taken by the conference. W E B DuBois was another great African American. He was a good friend of Tagore and Gandhi. What I mean is that the Black leaders of America were very interested in India's freedom struggle. But they did not pay any attention to the caste system. It is interesting that for them India as a whole was an example.

SL: That is because the whole of India was enslaved then, and they too were slaves. But now the rest of India is free while the Dalits are slaves. They may take an interest if they come to know about it.

AM: Yes. I have two other questions in mind. One question has been raised in a paper I read recently, by a young university professor. He says that sometimes the portrayal of Dalit life is rather romanticized. There is an effort to show a time when the caste system did not exist, or to imagine a society in which no one will have control over Dalit life. And that it will be a new society, completely different from today's society. This professor says that mostly savarna writers who have written about Dalits have engaged in this kind of writing. He compares it with a Dalit writer's work, which shows that while the writer regrets the loss of his traditions, he does not wish to live in the past. He wants to live in the new society that is being shaped. And he is writing about the compromises that have to be made for this purpose. This is a somewhat complex argument that he has proposed in his paper while discussing the Malayalam writer Narayan's novel *Koccharethi*. The novel deals with a seventy-year time span in the lives of an old man and an old woman from the Giriraja tribe of the Wayanad hills in Kerala. Narayan is a member of this tribe himself. The couple remember bygone days. Their daughter has taken up a government job and has made her peace with savarna society. They are saddened by this, but have also accepted it. This professor finds such a portrayal far more realistic compared to that of a savarna Malayalam writer, K J Baby, who in the novel, *Mavelimantram*, imagines that those who were slaves have staged a revolution and built a separate society in which there are no masters and the people are free. Based on this comparison, the critic is saying that Dalit writing is the writing of compromise. Do you think that thinking about the past or traditions is always tantamount to indulging in romanticism, and thinking about modernity means making compromises with the social order?

SL: Where is the compromise? Dalits have lived as slaves for thousands of years. He would be utterly wrong if he said that it would be non-compromise if they lived in slavery for another thousand years, or if they led a separate life. Of course, they have fought back. Until now, the fight between the two groups was a fight rooted in history, for separation even. The fight that is going on now, is a fight to become one. It is a fight to build a new society. And to the extent that it is a fight to create a new society, how can there be any compromise in it? This is precisely what this movement is about. There would have been no need for struggle if we only wanted to live separately. We can live apart, right? We have to live with the upper caste; this is why we have to fight with them. If we didn't want to coexist with them, there would be no question of a struggle. The struggle is for building a new inclusive society. We have to build a new social order in which the savarna as well as the untouchable will have changed. Both will become new. That is what this struggle is all about.

AM: My next question is related to the teaching of Dalit literature. Recently I was talking to another teacher. He said, 'What is there to teach in a text that makes self-evident points?' According to him, there is little teachable matter in a text that says, for example, that Black people are good and White people are bad. He said, 'I don't find much to teach in Dalit writings, even though I have great sympathy for them.' He felt that such a text could be dealt with in ten minutes because, what more would you do with it after you have said, 'See, how bad the actions of these people were, or how wrong this is, or how much pain we feel'?

SL: This thinking is wrong. Dalit writing is about lived realities. We will see that the literature that has come down to us from the age of *Ramayana* is about Ram. Even today, political parties here invoke the name of Ram. There are TV serials based on *Ramayana*, books on *Ramayana* continue to pour in. And the *Ramayana* is meditated upon in every temple. No one says that all this is about the same thing, because for them Ram is an important topic. The same is true of love. For years people have fallen in love with one another. Every day, so much love poetry and so many romantic novels are being written. There, too, because love is an important subject for those concerned, there is no accusation that this is monotonous. But when Dalits write about themselves, then it seems repetitious to these non-Dalits, because it is not an important topic for them. But it is not repetitive to Dalits. Just as writing about Ram does not seem repetitious to upper caste people, similarly writing about their own revolt does not seem repetitious to Dalits. Your second question is, what is teachable in this writing?

AM: Yes, there is an idea as to what is teachable. Take Shakespeare, for example, and why his works are 'classics', even though he too writes about love, about war, about which king was dethroned and which king was killed. I mean, if you look at it, his plots tend to be quite simple. But people go on teaching him. Why do they do it? They will answer: 'You will not tire of analyzing his language every time you teach him. You can keep on searching and digging endlessly for the images, the similes and the references to other people present in the work.'

SL: The thing is that Dalit literature cannot be taught in the way Shakespeare would be taught. Dalit literature cannot be evaluated the way in which we will evaluate Shakespeare's literature, classic literature. There are different approaches to evaluating literatures; there are different reasons for reading literature. Dalit literature has different approaches and methods. Literature can be studied from an aesthetic perspective, a psychological perspective, or a sociological perspective. Unlike classical literature, Dalit literature needs to be studied from a sociological perspective. If we look for classics in Dalit literature today, we won't find any. This literature deals with social problems, social order and social movements. And today, instead of teaching our youth classics, it is more important to teach them what a social movement is, what the social order is, and what our social problems are. Isn't it necessary to teach them about this social order and the philosophies of realism rather than classical literature, the heroes of which are kings and emperors? There are no kings and emperors in today's democratic society. Common people are the heroes of this democratic system. Today we should teach the language of the joys and sorrows, and rights and entitlements of common people in our schools and colleges. The old-fashioned thinking of those teachers who think that they are teachers of classics and that there are no classics in Dalit literature, must change. Until today you taught Shakespeare; it is necessary to teach that as a subject or a paper. It is important to teach the classics, Dalits should also read the classics. But it is also necessary to teach the literature of the Dalits from a sociological perspective. In order to understand Dalit literature, it is essential to understand the caste system here, the social problems here. Anyone who does not pay attention to the social order and the caste system that exist here, cannot understand Dalit literature. They will say things like, 'Where is the classic here?' This literature is concerned about the caste system that prevails, and that precisely is today's classic thought.

AM: I was also thinking that perhaps the professor has got this idea from his own training.

SL: There is another thing too. When was Sanskrit aesthetics written? When did Aristotle write? Has there been no change in the artistic values, the social order and the heroes of those days and of today? The literature that was written for kings and emperors, and the literature that had kings and emperors as heroes, and its aesthetic values, are simply not relevant for our times. The heroes of yesterday's literature were gods, it was the literature of the privileged. Dalits are absent in it. The literature of those who are untouchable, those who are downtrodden, cannot be measured with the artistic values of Shakespeare, it can only be assessed according to Ambedkarite thought and Dalit thought. Ambedkarite thought is the aesthetics of Dalit literature. This is exactly what I have written. I have written that this literature cannot be evaluated on the basis of either Sanskrit aesthetics or western aesthetics. The aesthetics of this literature can only be based on the thinking of Ambedkar and Phule. Has there ever been a revolution for love? In the history of the entire world, was a regime ever overthrown because of love? Was there bloodshed anywhere for love? There can be soirees for love, there can be poets' gatherings for love. But, there have been many struggles around the world for rights, entitlements and equality. Yes, there have been many revolutions, many people have been martyred. Isn't it madness that when a boy and a girl visit a garden, the narrative becomes a classic, but when the writing is about thousands who sacrifice themselves for their freedom, who fight to put an end to their slavery, it is not considered to be a classic?

AM: Many people have assumptions about what should be considered literature. If Dalit literature does not fit their assumptions they will say that it is not worth teaching.

SL: Romantic youth will not like Dalit literature, and activists involved in movements will not like romantic literature. But both are part of the society. It is important to teach romantic literature just as it is important to teach Dalit literature. When there are people studying literature, all kinds of literature should be taught. 'I shall only read this literature and not that literature, and I shall teach this literature in my class and not that', is wrong thinking. All methods, all forms and all literary purposes should be included.

AM: I have seen the English curriculum of several universities. These days Indian literature in translation is being taught. However, although Mahasweta Devi and Mulk Raj Anand have been included, the same is not true of Dalit literature. I wonder to what extent the view that this professor expressed to me is responsible for this situation.

SL: The body that prepares the framework and designs syllabuses in universities, and decides which literature should be taught, is motivated by an ideology that is not progressive. In the old days, students and teachers came from a particular caste. Literature was created specifically for them. The textbooks were written only for them and were studied only by them. So far, there has not been a major change in this arrangement. A new consciousness is emerging among people, including the syllabus makers. Progressive people, of whom there is just a handful, are fighting that syllabuses should include Dalit literature. Right now, a Dalit flavour is included as an example, as a sample. There is another aspect to this—Dalit literature has not yet appeared in English translation. What little has appeared does not fit the accepted notion of classic literature. Therefore, it is being removed. If someone considers a certain Dalit work to be a classic, and has translated it, or his relative has done the translation, then he will include it in the syllabus and say that it should be taught. Much of Dalit literature is to be found in the regional languages and has to be translated into English on a massive scale. An entire pool, a huge stream, will have to be created, and a debate should be provoked. Only then can Dalit literature be paid due attention. Right now, a lot of work is being done on Dalit literature in the regional universities; Dalit literature is being taught there. In Maharashtra, for example, Dalit literature is taught from primary school to the university level.

AM: You were saying that the first theoretical discussions happened in Milind College. When did that happen, in which year?

SL: This discussion took place in 1967. This was the first discussion with reference to Dalit literature: What should Dalit literature be? How should it be written? Progressive savarna thinkers and critics were present. At that time, they proposed many names for Dalit literature. Some called it revolt literature, other suggested neo-Buddhist literature. We have many scheduled castes; among these Babasaheb's community is neo-Buddhist. It is the leading community. The discussion of a representative Dalit literature took place in the context of this leading neo-Buddhist community. A body of representative literature had not yet been written; it had only begun to be produced at that time. What happened is that, on one hand, Dalit literature had just begun to be written and, on the other hand, its criticism was already being constructed. In terms of the development of Dalit literature, it seems to me that criticism came first and literature later. And, yes, it is progressive savarna critics who worked to develop Dalit literature. They supported it, and encouraged people to write. And so it began.

The literature of Dalit writers was ultimately called Dalit literature. The word Dalit was meant to signify the oppressed. Then several critics who were Dalits by birth rejected this word out of concern that this movement would become communist and stray from the path of Ambedkarism. They argued that instead of Dalit literature it should be called Buddhist literature because they had become Buddhists and were no longer Dalits. The term Buddhist literature was used instead of Dalit literature. Buddhist literary conferences began to take place. The same writers who used to come to Dalit literature conferences were now going to Buddhist literature conferences. Yes, the same Sharankumar Limbale was going to Buddhist as well as to Dalit literature conferences! But, what they were writing as Dalits, the history that they were talking about, did not include Buddhism.

What I mean is, it was a literature that talked about the kind of injustices and excesses that were committed against Dalits. This literature was concerned with the incidents that were related to casteism rather than with Buddhism. Hence the term Buddhist was set aside within a decade, while Dalit remained. Even so, the proponents of the term Buddhist tried once again to oppose the use of the word Dalit: 'Instead of Dalit, we should use the term Ambedkarite and call it Ambedkarite literature, like Marxist literature. By calling it Dalit literature, we are not paying attention to – we are neglecting – the inspiration that comes from Ambedkar.' This kind of a discussion began, and those who preferred the term Dalit were accused of being Communists and were removed from the movement. As a result, everyone engaged in Dalit writing, those who were Dalits, or Ambedkarites, or supporters of Buddhism, said, 'Our inspiration is Ambedkar.' It became a fashion to say, 'Only Ambedkar is my inspiration.' Every writer said this, and it continues to be said today.

It was possible to make such a declaration because people from only one community were writing during that period. Only people from Ambedkarji's community were writing, and they were leading the Dalit literary and social movements. Therefore, the debate was taking place only amongst them. When people from communities other than Dr Ambedkar's Mahar community came into the movement in large numbers – people like Laxman Gaikwad, Lakshman Mane, Madhav Kondvilkar, Kishor Kale and Ashok Pawar, people who had led lives even more frightening than those of the Mahars – and started writing, the discussion of the literature of Mahars took a back seat. The question arose: 'If the literature of the Mahar community is called neo-Buddhist literature, what shall we call the literature of the non-Mahar Dalits?'

So, Dalit was the correct term for a broad definition—thus the word gained acceptance. Even today there are many people who are opposed to the label Dalit literature. There was also an argument: 'If there are objections to using only Ambedkar, then add Phule to Ambedkar and call it Phule–Ambedkar literature.' In any case, Buddhist literature became isolated, and is now almost non-existent. Buddhist literature includes religious literature, it is connected to the literature that exists in Pali, such as the *Jatakas*. The suffering that the Buddha observed when he saw a corpse, an old person and a beggar, made him run away. If the Buddha had seen the suffering of the untouchable, he would perhaps have committed suicide, right? It is such an extreme suffering, and Dalit writers have now begun to write about this suffering. So, after non-Mahar writers began to write, the word Dalit gained ascendancy.

AM: Has there been any discussion about these matters since 1967? Now there is a large body of Dalit writing. Have savarna and Dalit critics come together for any kind of examination of the work that has been done?

SL: You've asked me a very good question. Such a discussion has not happened. I mentioned it even yesterday. People who believe in progressive ideas are almost non-existent today. There is bitterness between the Dalit and the humanistic movements. Just as a sharp revolt has entered the Dalit movement, in reaction to it, the minds and hearts of the savarna people have become embittered. And, caught between the revolt and the bitterness, progressive thought has disappeared. Savarnas are becoming aggressive in direct proportion to the degree of aggressiveness in Dalits. As a result of these two aggressive communalisms, the progressive dialogue that existed has vanished. How can there be movement forward, where there is no dialogue? That is why, today, Dalit literature is becoming static. Obviously, aggressive Dalits cannot engage in dialogue with aggressive savarnas. But the break in the dialogue has caused great harm to the Dalit literary movement. This is how I feel after three decades.

AM: So, tell me, what are the conditions like at this moment? What do you think is the type of work that needs to be done in this context?

SL: It seems to me that at this moment, there is a need to bring together the Dalits and the progressive savarnas. Only by joining hands will they be able to uproot the forces that are propagating the thought of Manu among Dalits as well as savarnas. Without that, it appears difficult to maintain dialogue and I fear that dialogue has been terminated.

AM: I had asked you yesterday whether there is any difference in your writing since you wrote *Akkarmashi*. What do you think has been the effect on your writing of the conditions that are now coming to the fore?

SL: Oh, a great deal! I was twenty-five years old when I wrote *Akkarmashi*. Today, when I am forty-five, I have written *Akkarmashi* once again. The experiences, the literary understanding and the social interpretation that I had when I was twenty-five have expanded greatly. The other aspect is the difference between the conditions today and at that time. When I was writing back then, the mood of the Dalit movement was very positive and progressive tendencies were working hand-in-hand with it. The two decades between 1960 and 1980 were very good for the Dalit movement. After we wrote our books, there used to be a lot of immediate discussion. Writers were revered, and there used to be many literary festivals and conferences. Everything was seen with a good, positive attitude. The environment today is no longer what it was in 1960s, '70s and '80s. And it seems to me that just before the beginning of the twenty-first century, around 1985, after the BJP–Shiv Sena coalition formed governments in the state and the centre, the situation became very delicate.

Then, there is the issue of globalization. Today, there is an anti-Dalit government in this state as well as at the centre, and talk of globalization has begun. All these events have confronted the Dalit movement quite suddenly. These developments had not been visualized and, therefore, the activists involved in the movement are somewhat nonplussed. This situation has also forced me to rethink. So, when I wrote the novel *Upalya*, I wrote about the politics of the Congress and the Republican Party of India. I wrote about the four decades from 1956 to 1996. When I was writing the last few pages of the novel, I would hesitate, I used to pause as to what I should write about RPI and Congress, when a Shiv Sena–BJP government was working in the province and at the centre. Concerned about the effect of my writing on the situation, I was forced reluctantly to mention them as well. If this had not been the case, I would not have mentioned them, that is, if I'd been able to write freely. There has also been a change in my normally sharp temper.

AM: You have written at least thirty books in the last twenty-five years. In *Akkarmashi*, you captured one particular period of time, and in *Upalya*, your most recent novel, you have written about what has happened in these twenty-five years. Please give me an overview of your writing over these twenty-five years.

SL: There has been change. When I first started writing, I used to write on an imaginative level. When I was studying in school, my Kaka was the head of the village and he was an orthodox savarna and he gave me books to read—*Ramayana, Mahabharata, Bhagvad Gita*. I read all the sacred texts of the Hindus, and I read them in elementary school. This had such an impact on my mind that all the time, even while sleeping, I used to recite the names of gods, I used to constantly take the names of all the Hindu gods, I used to say, 'Jai Bhavani, Jai Bhavani'. The Hindu religion was present all over my notebooks and books. Sometimes, I felt that I should renounce everything, go to the Himalayas and be an ascetic, become a Shankaracharya. That's the kind of effect these works had on my child mind.

Afterwards, when I left home to go to a boarding school, I met students from different communities and the majority among them were Dalit boys. This was in the high school which was quite near our village, and my transformation began in that school. Later, in the college hostel, there were boys from many different communities and they brought with them many different cultures. The majority of the boys were Dalits, who invoked the name of Babasaheb Ambedkar. I began to fight with them. I used to take the name of god and they took the name of Babasaheb. In these fights, I found myself completely isolated. I began to think and question myself. Thereafter, my life in college went into searching for, recognizing and reforming myself. The boys were very militant and they were fighting against the caste spirit. There, I was not just completely isolated, they would even threaten to beat me up. They would say, 'You get your job through reservation, you take money from reservation, you get to study due to reservation and you say "Namaskar"! Why don't you say "Jai Bhim"? You say "Ambedkar", why don't you say "Babasaheb"?' I have written about this in *Akkarmashi*. They beat me into recognizing myself, that this is the real me. And there I changed a little.

Later, I got a job and went to the Marathwada region where the movement to rename Marathwada University after Dr Babasaheb Ambedkar began. I had arrived there a couple of years before the movement began. The movement continued for fifteen years, progressively becoming violent and aggressive. I found my true identity through that movement. Until then, I'd only written love poetry. I used to write under the influence of white-collar writers, the middle-class writers writing here. Then, after I joined that movement, I tore it all up. I had written at least fifty manuscripts, which included poetry, plays and stories. I burned all of them. 'All of this is sheer nonsense. It's all imagination. My real self is not in them, my questions are not in them, my understanding is not in them, my movement is not in them.' This is how it seemed to me. My wife said, 'Please let them be.

I shall read them after you go to the office.' I replied, 'No, these are useless!'

After that movement, I found my true voice. The first movement, about which we talked yesterday, was about the past. When I wrote *Akkarmashi*, I too wrote about the past. My past was in it and I was only looking at the past. Now, after twenty-five years, my past has been so destroyed that I have been cut off from it, I've been completely separated from it. Neither have I gone home, nor does my mother see me as I was before. 'Some big officer has come, some VIP guest has come': thus will she offer me water. I no longer have the same attachment to my colony, my relatives, my language. Everything has changed. And because of that change, I am done writing about the history that I had to write about.

What has happened now in Dalit writing is that those who have written about history, about the past, and have not thought about the future, they have come to a standstill, they have stopped. The raw material for their writing is exhausted. There is no road ahead. Those who are thinking about today, about the future, they are writing. Seventy-five per cent of the new writers who are coming forward are writing about the past and the other twenty-five per cent are experimenting with form, trying to bring literary value into it. They are not thinking about today or tomorrow. This is where Dalit literature has stopped, it seems to me. To take this literature forward, today's Dalit writers have to think about the present and about the future. The present is so frightening, so new, that I can't even fathom it.

Let me say one thing: since last year I have been living in this building where I own this flat. In the building, there is a Christian family, a Muslim family, and a Maratha family. And all these children come to my house, and my children visit every house for the Satyanarayana ceremony and birthdays. The social system in the context of which we were thinking – I was not allowed to take water; I was not allowed to enter the temple; The barber did not cut my hair; Nobody touched me – has changed. Now, there is a tap in the kitchen of my house, there are taps in the bathroom, there is a tap in the toilet, okay? My children are not aware of the extreme nature of that struggle. Whenever I tell my children that I came out of extreme poverty, that many times I had nothing to eat, they think that I am mad, that I am talking nonsense. If my father or grandfather had said the same to me, I would have believed them. But today my children will not believe that I have experienced poverty. Even my mother will not believe that I was poor. The conditions that I have written about, the environment that I have written about, no longer exist in my house, because of the position that I happen to hold today. Today, my daughter has had an inter-caste marriage. Now Dada, my daughter's father-in-law, and I can sit here and talk like father and son. Twenty-five years ago, I would not have thought so much change was possible. But conditions are changing and they will continue to change. However, no one has thought about this changing environment. Such reflection is necessary, it has to be undertaken. When we begin to adopt such a perspective, the shape of Dalit literature will become quite different. Such thinking needs to be undertaken.

AM: I have read some Hindi stories recently and from them it seems that there is some effort to explore what kinds of issues Dalits face, now that they have made some progress, have become IAS officers. I haven't seen too many of these stories, only a few. Yet, it seems that the environment depicted in them is still one of untouchability. But you are saying that the environment is changing.

SL: Well, when there is a war the captain has to always stay focused. Literature is not a verbatim portrayal of society. The message should be: 'You are slaves. You must battle against your slavery.' In any case, the purpose of Dalit literature has always been to struggle against this caste system. That is why every picture, even if it is that of Mona Lisa, will have to be portrayed in this context. From whatever source and in whichever way, the idea of fighting against this system will have to be brought in, whether it is the experience of an IAS officer, or as I said yesterday, that of the president of the country. When we look at the characters peopling the writing, we will see them in terms of this social order, and that is the sole objective of Dalit literature. If we forget this, it will disappear. We want to keep it alive so long as this caste system is alive. And that is why it is said that we are posturing as writers, that we are not neutral. Whenever Dalit writers write, they have a role in mind, a clear intention. Consequently, when they portray society they don't just portray society, their own role is very much a part of this process—the role of opposing the caste system.

AM: In many of the stories that I read in your collection *Devta Aadmi*, I noticed that the main character is a writer. The protagonist of *Upalya* is also a writer. Why do you use the figure of the writer as your central character?

SL: This is a big limitation of mine. You mentioned *Upalya*. When I wrote the first draft, it was in the third person. When I wrote *Akkarmashi* it got a lot of publicity and a lot of praise. Since then, I liked using the autobiographical form to express myself. It is very expressive. It originates with the 'I', that is my experience, my finding of my voice. I don't have to change my way of writing a lot while using this form. Writing in the third person is different. In it, someone else is speaking, someone else is doing something. But my writing starts with me and I just cannot separate my writing from me. I began with *Akkarmashi*, and since it got so much praise, I decided that I would use this form exclusively. I have been trying to remove myself from my writing, but I have not been successful.

AM: You talked about neutrality, so this is my last question. A few days ago, the writer U R Anantamurthy was talking about modernism in Hyderabad. He was saying that in modernist literature, the writer is only a witness, he cannot be committed. He claimed that Dalit writing is modernist writing. Do you think that the Dalit writer is a neutral witness?

SL: No, never! A Dalit writer cannot be neutral. When injustice is being done to my mother and my sister, I cannot sit still. When a house is burning down, I'm not going to remain silent. This happens in literature too. The writer can be neutral only when there is no relationship between him and experience; when he is manufacturing new experiences from imagination and skill. In Dalit literature, writers are narrating their own experiences, they are writing about their own society. Whatever is in this literature, it is theirs, they cannot remain neutral. To be neutral can be very damaging to Dalit literature and the Dalit movement. If Dalit writers remain neutral, they'll become pessimistic. They have to take sides. They will not fulfil their artistic responsibility simply by recording or reporting. Dalit literature is action and they have to engage in action, and it is only through writers being activists that Dalit literature can stay alive. Laxman Gaikwad is an activist, this is why we read his work with such affection. When we expel the activist from the writer, he is no longer a Dalit writer. A Dalit writer must possess a particular consciousness. Yes, he must have commitment. When we remove consciousness and commitment, he will no longer be a Dalit writer. Therefore, the primary requirements for Dalit writers is that they must be committed to their society and they must have Dalit consciousness in their hearts and minds. It is the upper castes who attempt to mislead by saying that a classic is that work which is objective or neutral. We must guard against being misled.

Glossary

Abhang	A form of spiritual poetry in Marathi.
Adivasi	Aboriginal peoples of India, usually forest dwellers.
Ashtang marg	Eight principles of life according to Buddhism.
Asmitadarsh	Dalit literary magazine started in 1967 by Gangadhar Pantawane from Aurangabad, Maharashtra. For the last 34 years, it has recognized and published Dalit writing. First started as *Asmita*, but refused registration, subsequently registered as *Asmitadarsh*, it provided an outlet for Dalit writing when others refused to publish. The magazine also launched the annual Asmitadarsh Dalit literary conferences.
Avtarvad	Principle of incarnation, found in both Hinduism and Buddhism.
Basti	Settlement.
Chamar	Cobbler; name of an untouchable caste.
Dalitva	Dalitness; the essence of being Dalit.
Harijan	The people of god/Hari; a term used to refer to untouchables, popularized by Mahatma Gandhi.
Jai Bhim	Victory to Babasaheb Bhimrao Ambedkar; a greeting used by followers of Babasaheb.
Jalsa	Presentation of Ambedkarite movement in folk drama form.
Kabir	A fourteenth–fifteenth century Hindi poet, who believed in mysticism and wrote against the negative aspects of Hinduism as well as Islam. A weaver by profession, he is believed to have been the son of a Hindu mother, raised by a Muslim weaver family. Dalits regard him as one of their own.
Karmasiddhant	Buddhist principle of right conduct.
Mahanirvan	Great departure; reference to the passing away of Babasaheb Ambedkar.

Mohalla	Neighbourhood.
Moksha	Hindu concept of release from the cycle of rebirth.
Mooknayak	1. Leader of the mute; reference to Babasaheb Ambedkar. 2. Name of the weekly started by Babasaheb Ambedkar.
Nautanki	A form of popular entertainment in which stories of love and romance are dramatized through dance and song.
Neo-Buddhist	Dalit converts to Buddhism. As a protest against the oppressive practices and tenets of Hinduism, Dr Ambedkar advocated mass conversion of Dalits to Buddhism.
Nirvana	Buddhist concept of release from the cycle of death and rebirth.
Nomadic and criminal tribes	Itinerant communities with no fixed place, considered criminal by birth and pushed out of the village. There are a total of forty-two nomadic and criminal tribes, some of which peddled general stores, others engaged in street entertainment, and yet others begged and engaged in petty theft for livelihood.
Panchasheel	Five rules of Buddhist moral conduct.
Phule	Mahatma Jotirao Phule (1827–1890).
Prakrit	Literal meaning: natural or without artifice. As opposed to Sanskrit, which is the medium for expressing the divine word and is, therefore, the language of the Aryas, that is, the civilized people, Prakrit is the language of the non-Arya.
Rasa	Literal meaning: juice; Sanskrit aesthetic concept.
Rural literature	School or tradition of literary writing that drew its inspiration, subject, themes and characters from rural life. As initially practised by bourgeois urban writers, rural literature romanticized rural life, not unlike the European Romantics. A more realistic trend developed with the emergence of writers who themselves hailed from the village.
Sangha	Order of Buddhist bhikkus or monks.
Sanskaras	Rituals.
Sanskriti	Culture, refinement.

Sant	A pious person; an ascetic; often a writer of religious/spiritual/mystical poetry.
Sant literature	Devotional literature – mostly poetry and songs – composed by Hindu religious personalities.
Savarna	Literal meaning: with varna; referring to those who belong to the four varnas (see below). However, the term 'savarna' is popularly used to refer to upper caste people.
SC/ST	Abbreviations for Scheduled Caste and Scheduled Tribe. These are official lists of castes and tribes that are recognized by the Constitution of India as being historically disadvantaged. These castes and tribes are called scheduled because of their inclusion in a Schedule of the Constitution.
Separate riverbanks	Upper caste people went to the highest point of the river to draw water, bathe, wash clothes, etc, other backward people went further down the river, and Dalits remained at the lowest point.
Sikkhapad	Teachings of Buddhism.
Southborough Commission	A commission established in 1919 under the chairmanship of Lord Southborough to deal with franchise problems arising out of the Montagu–Chelmsford Report on Indian Constitutional Reforms. Invited to give evidence before this commission, Babasaheb Ambedkar demanded separate electorates and reserved seats for the depressed classes in proportion to their population.
Trisharan	Three shelters according to Buddha.
Varna	Literally means colour, it is the Sanskrit nomenclature for the original division of Hindu society into four castes—Brahmana, Kshatriya, Vaishya and Shudra. It is the foundation of Hinduism.
Vihar	Buddhist temple.

Works Cited

Aachwal, Madhav. 1972. *Rasaswad: Wangmay ani Samiksha*. Bombay: Mumbai Marathi Sahitya Sangha.

Ahmad, Aijaz. 1992. 'Jameson's Rhetoric of Otherness and the 'National Allegory'.' In *In Theory: Classes, Nations, Literatures*. London: Verso. 95–122.

Ambedkar, Babasaheb. 1927a. *Bahishkrit Bharat*, 3 April 1927.

——. 1927b. *Bahishkrit Bharat*, 3 June 1927.

——. 1927c. *Bahishkrit Bharat*, 29 July 1927.

——. 1928a. *Bahishkrit Bharat*, 3 February 1928.

——. 1928b. *Samata*, 5 October 1928.

——. 1929a. *Bahishkrit Bharat*, 1 February 1929.

——. 1929b. *Bahishkrit Bharat*, 4 December 1929.

——. 1938. GIP Railway Workers' Conference, 12 February 1938.

——. 1944. Daily *Sakal*, 30 November 1944.

——. 1947. Daily *Navyug*, 13 April 1947.

——. 1976. Souvenir. Nagpur: Dalit Sahitya Sammelan.

——. 1987. *Buddha or Karl Marx*. n.d. In *Dr. Babasaheb Ambedkar: Writings and Speeches*. Vol. 3. Compiled by Vasant Moon. Bombay: Education Department, Government of Maharashtra.

——. [1979] 1989. *Annihilation of Caste with a Reply to Mahatma Gandhi*. (1936; 1944). In *Dr. Babasaheb Ambedkar: Writings and Speeches*. Vol. 1. Compiled by Vasant Moon. Bombay: Education Department, Government of Maharashtra.

——. [1948] 1990. *The Untouchables: Who were they and Why they became Untouchables?* In *Dr. Babasaheb Ambedkar: Writings and Speeches*. Vol. 7. Ed. Vasant Moon. Bombay: Education Department, Government of Maharashtra.

Anand, Mulk Raj, and Eleanor Zelliot, eds. 1992. *An Anthology of Dalit Literature (Poems)*. New Delhi: Gyan Publishing House.

Bagul, Baburao. 1980. *Dalit Sahitya: Aajche Kranti Vigyan*. Nagpur: Buddhist Publishing House.

Baker, Jr., Houston A, ed. 1976. *Reading Black: Essays in the Criticism of African, Caribbean, and Black American Literature*. Cornell University

Africana Studies and Research Center Monograph Series, no. 4. University of Pennsylvania, Afro-American Studies Program, and Cornell University Africana Studies and Research Center.

Bakhtin, M M. 1981. *The Dialogic Imagination: Four Essays.* Edited by Michael Holquist. Translated by Caryl Emerson and Michael Holquist. Austin: University of Texas Press.

Bhabha, Homi K. 1994. *The Location of Culture.* London and New York: Routledge.

Bharadwaj, Hetu. 1998. 'Ghaatak Nahin Hogaa Sahitya kaa Yeh Vibhaajan?' ('Won't This Division of Literature be Fatal?'). *Hans*, March, 35–36.

Brooks, Gwendolyn. 1969. Introduction to *Black Words That Say: Don't Cry, Scream.* By Don L Lee. Detroit: Broadside Press. 9–13.

Chapekar, N G. *Nivedak Lekh.* Bhag Ek. [Details not available]

Chendwankar, Prahlad. 1976. 'Mi Mhanato.' In *Audit*. Bombay: Abhinav Prakashan.

Chitnis, M B. [1978] 1998. 'Maharashtratil Aaj-Udyacha Sanskritik Sangharsh ani Wangmayin Samasya.' Discussion, Milind College, Aurangabad, 16–24 November 1967. *Asmita*. First issue. Aurangabad, 1967. Reprinted in Arjun Dangle, ed., *Dalit Sahitya: Ek Abhyas*. Pune: Sugawa Prakashan.

Dangle, Arjun, ed. [1992] 1994. *A Corpse in the Well: Translations from Modern Marathi Dalit Autobiographies.* Hyderabad: Orient Longman.

Deshpande, Kusumavati. 1987. *Pasang.* Bombay: Mauj Prakashan.

Dhale, Raja. 1992. Presidential Speech, Shatabdi Sahitya Sammelan, 18–19 January 1992.

Dhasal, Namdeo. 1973. 'Dalit Panthercha Jahirnama.' Pamphlet, 1972. Reprinted in Baburao Bagul, ed., *Aamhi*, Diwali Annual.

Fanon, Frantz. 1967. *Black Skin, White Masks.* Translated by Charles Lam Markmann. New York: Grove Weidenfeld.

——. [1968] 1979. *The Wretched of the Earth.* Foreword by Jean-Paul Sartre. Translated by Constance Farrington. New York: Grove Press.

Freibert, Stuart, and David Young, eds. 1989. *The Longman Anthology of Contemporary American Poetry: 1950 to the Present.* 2nd edn. New York and London: Longman.

Gaekwad, Baburao. 1986. *Drishtikshep.* Aurangabad: Parichay Prakashan.

Garvey, Marcus. 1972a. 'An Appeal to the Conscience of the Black Race to See Itself.' In Richard A Long and Eugenia W Collier, eds., *Afro-American Writing: An Anthology of Prose and Poetry.* Vol. 2. New York: New York University Press. 365–371.

——. 1972b. 'The Principles of the Universal Negro Improvement

Association.' Speech Delivered at Liberty Hall, 25 November 1922. In Richard A Long and Eugenia W Collier, eds., *Afro-American Writing: An Anthology of Prose and Poetry*. Vol. 2. New York: New York University Press. 356–364.

Gautam, Roopchand. 1996. 'Dalit Sahitya Par Aur Bhi Bahas Jaroori Hai' ('Even More Debate about Dalit Literature is Essential'). *Hans*, November, 79.

Gayle, Jr., Addison. 1976. 'The Function of Black Criticism at the Present Time.' In Houston A Baker, Jr., ed., *Reading Black: Essays in the Criticism of African, Caribbean, and Black American Literature*. Cornell University Africana Studies and Research Center Monograph Series, no. 4. 37–40.

Gorky, Maxim. 1982. Vol. 10 of *Collected Works in Ten Volumes. On Literature*. Moscow: Progress Publishers.

Hirschkop, Ken. 1992. 'Is Dialogism for Real?' *Social Text* 30, 102–113.

Hogan, Patrick Colm, and Lalita Pandit, eds. 1995. *Literary India: Comparative Studies in Aesthetics, Colonialism, and Culture*. Albany: State University of New York Press.

Jack, Belinda Elizabeth. 1996. *Negritude and Literary Criticism: The History and Theory of 'Negro-African' Literature in French*. Westport, Conn.: Greenwood Press.

Jameson, Frederic. 1986. 'Third-World Literature in the Era of Multinational Capitalism.' *Social Text* 15, 65–88.

Joshi, R Barbara, ed. *Untouchable! Voices of the Dalit Liberation Movement*. London: Zed Books.

Kawthekar, Balkrishna. 1981. *Dalit Sahitya: Ek Aakalan*. Kolhapur: Ajab Pustakalay.

Keer, Dhananjay. [1971] 1987. *Dr. Ambedkar: Life and Mission*. 3rd edn. Bombay: Popular Prakashan.

Khandekar, Tarachandra. 1981. *Ambedkar Tatwagyan: Prachiti ani Awishkar*. Nagpur: Prabha Prakashan.

Kharpade, D K. 1990. *Bahujan Sangram*, (November–December).

Killens, John O. 1972. 'The Black Psyche.' In Richard A Long and Eugenia W Collier, eds., *Afro-American Writing: An Anthology of Prose and Poetry*. Vol 2. New York: New York University Press. 609–618.

Kulikova, I, and A Zis, eds. 1976. *Marxist-Leninist Aesthetics and Life: A Collection of Articles*. Moscow: Progress Publishers.

Kulkarni, G M. [1979] 1984. 'Prastavana.' In Anand Yadav, *Gramin Sahitya: Swarup ani Samasya*. Pune: Mehta Publishing House.

Kulkarni, V L. [1978] 1998. 'Maharashtratil Aaj-Udyacha Sanskritik

Sangharsh ani Wangmayin Samasya.' Discussion, Milind College, Aurangabad, 16–24 November 1967. *Asmita*. First issue. Aurangabad, 1967. Reprinted in Arjun Dangle, ed., *Dalit Sahitya: Ek Abhyas*. Pune: Sugawa Prakashan.

Kurundkar, Narhar. 1981. *Bhajan*. Pune: Srividya Prakashan.

Leizerov, A. 1976. 'The Birth of a New Art.' In I Kulikova and A Zis, eds., *Marxist-Leninist Aesthetics and Life: A Collection of Articles*. Moscow: Progress Publishers. 155–166.

Limbale, Sharankumar. 1994. '*Akkarmashi* ki Janmapatri' ('*Akkarmashi*'s Horoscope'). Translated by Surya Narayan Ransubhe. *Hans*, March, 32–37.

———. 1997. 'Dalit Saahitya: Swarup aur Prayojan' ('Dalit Literature: Form and Purpose'). *Hans*, January, 52–55.

———. 1885. Humay Daya Nahin Adhikar Chahiye: Sharankumar Limbale (We Want Rights Not Pity: Sharankumar Limbale). Interview by Omprakash Valmiki. *Hans*, December, 33–35.

Mande, Prabhakar. 1979. *Dalit Sahityache Niralapan*. Aurangabad: Dhara Prakashan.

Manohar, Yashwant. 1978. *Dalit Sahitya: Siddhant ani Swarup*. Aurangabad: Waman Nimbalkar, Prabodhan Prakashan.

———. 1988. *Dalit Sahitya Chintan*. Nagpur: Sanghamitra Book House.

Marx, Karl, and Frederick Engels. 1947. *Literature and Art: Selections from their Writings*. New York: International Publishers.

McKay, Claude. 1970. *A Long Way from Home: An Autobiography*. New York: Lee Furman Inc, 1937. Reprint with Introduction by St. Clair Drake. New York: Harcourt, Brace.

Moon, Vasant. 1982. Presidential Address. Asmitadarsh Literary Conference, Ulhasnagar.

Mukherjee, Arun. 1998. *Postcolonialism: My Living*. Toronto: TSAR.

Muktibodh, Sharatchandra. 1986. Response to Questionnaire. In G M Kulkarni, ed., *Dalit Sahitya: Pravah ani Pratikriya*. Pune: Pratima Prakashan.

Naimishray, Mohan Dass. 1993. 'Stree Aarambh se Ant tak Dalit Hee Hai' ('Woman is a Dalit from Beginning to End'). *Hans*, September, 75.

Nautiyal, Vidyasagar. 1993. '*Akkarmashi*: Dalit Jwalamukhi' ('*Akkarmashi*: Dalit Volcano'). *Hans*, April, 74–76.

Palsikar, Vasant. 1986. Response to Questionnaire. In G M Kulkarni, ed., *Dalit Sahitya: Pravah ani Pratikriya*. Pune: Pratima Prakashan.

Pandey, Bhavdev. 1996. 'Hindi Sahitya kaa Savarna Itihaas: Nahin, Yeh

Jaativad Nahin Hai' ('Caste History of Hindi Literature: No, This is Not Casteism'). *Hans*, October, 77–78.

Patil, M S. 1981. *Dalit Kavita*. Bombay: Lokwangmay Griha Ltd.

Patil, Sharad. 1988. *Abrahmani Sahityanche Saundaryashastra*. Pune: Sugawa Prakashan.

Pawar, Daya. 1987. *Baluta Ek Vadal*. Bombay: Rohan Prakashan.

———. 1990. In Vilas Patil, ed., *Bhui kote*. Diwali Annual.

Phadke, N S. *Pratibha Vilas*. [Details not available]

Phadkule, Nirmalkumar. 1986. *Kahi Rang: Kahi Resha*. Pune: Mehta Publishing House.

Poddar, A, ed. 1972. *Indian Literature: Proceedings of a Seminar*. Shimla: Indian Institute of Advanced Studies.

Ranade, Pandharinath. 1991. Daily *Lokmat*, 21 July 1991.

Raosaheb, Mohan. 1990. *Bahujan Sangram*, (November–December).

Redding, J Saunders. 1976. 'Afro-American Culture and the Black Aesthetic: Notes toward a Re-Evaluation.' In Houston A Baker, Jr., ed., *Reading Black: Essays in the Criticism of African, Caribbean, and Black American Literature*. Cornell University Africana Studies and Research Center Monograph Series, no. 4. 41–47.

Rege, P S. 1968. *Chandsi*. 2nd edn. Bombay: Mauj Prakashan.

Sardesai, S G. 1979. *Class Struggle and Caste Conflict in Rural Areas*. Communist Party Publication no.14. New Delhi: Communist Party of India.

Sharma, Ramvilas. 1981. *Paramparaa kaa Mulyankan*. New Delhi: Rajkamal Prakashan.

Sonwane, Vijay. 1979. *Dalit Sahitya ka Nako?* Foreword by Bhausaheb Adsul. Aurangabad: Maharashtra Boudha Sahitya Parishad.

Soyinka, Wole. 1976. 'Aesthetic Illusions.' In Houston A. Baker, Jr., ed., *Reading Black: Essays in the Criticism of African, Caribbean, and Black American Literature*. Cornell University Africana Studies and Research Center Monograph Series, no. 4. 1–12.

Spivak, Gayatri Chakravorty. 1988. 'Draupadi by Mahasweta Devi.' In *In Other Worlds: Essays in Cultural Politics*. New York: Routledge. 179–196.

Thatte, Yadunath. 1990. *Yugvani*. (April–June).

Tripathi, Shailendra Kumar. 1988. 'Dalit Chintan Banaam Itihaas' ('Dalit Thinking versus History'). *Hans*. July, 68.

Tupe, Uttam Bandhu. 1983. *Asmitadarsh: Atmakatha Visheshanka*. Diwali Annual.

Waghmare, Janardan. 1992. 'Black Literature and Dalit Literature.' In

Arjun Dangle, ed., *Poisoned Bread: Translations from Modern Marathi Dalit Literature.* Hyderabad: Orient Longman. 305–314.

Wankhede, M N. 1981. *Dalitanche Vidrohi Wangmay.* Nagpur: Prabodhan Prakashan.

Young, Robert J C. 1995. *Colonial Desire: Hybridity in Theory, Culture and Race.* London: Routledge.

Further Reading: A Select List of Dalit Literature

ALOK MUKHERJEE

The following select list of literary, critical and historical writing available in English is provided for anyone interested in further reading. In addition to my own resources, I have drawn on the research of Anand Mahanand, Arun Mukherjee and Eleanor Zelliot to compile this list. I am thankful to them.

A. LITERATURE

Ambedkar, B R. 2003. *Ambedkar: Autobiographical Notes*. Introduction by Ravikumar. Pondicherry: Navayana.

Bama. 2000. *Karukku*. Translated by Lakshmi Holmstrom. Chennai: Macmillan.

Bhagat, Datta. 1994. 'Routes and Escape-Routes.' Translated by Maya Pandit. In Satish Alekar, ed., *Yatra: Writings from the Indian Subcontinent 3*. New Delhi: Indus.

———. 2000. 'Whirlwind.' Translated by Georg Naggies, Vimal Thorat and Eleanor Zelliot. In G P Deshpande, ed., *Indian Drama since 1950*. New Delhi: Sahitya Akademi.

Devanoor, Mahadeva. 1992. 'Tar Arrives.' Translated by Manu Shetty and A K Ramanujan. In *From Cavery to Godavari: Modern Kannada Short Stories*. New Delhi: Penguin.

Gaikwad, Laxman. 1998. *The Branded*. Translated by P A Kolharkar. New Delhi: Sahitya Akademi.

Gajvi, Premanand. 2000. Interview and excerpts from *Ghotbhar Pani*. In Shanta Gokhale, ed., *Playwright at the Centre: Marathi Drama—from 1843 to the Present*. Kolkata: Seagull.

Hazari. [1951] 1969. *Untouchable: The Autobiography of an Indian Outcaste*. New York: Frederick A. Praeger.

Imayam. 2001. *Beasts of Burden*. Translated by Lakshmi Holmstrom. Chennai: Manas.

Jadhav, Narendra. 2003. *Outcaste: A Memoir*. New Delhi: Penguin.

Jilthe, Manohar. 1992. *Parched Heart*. Aurangabad: Veluvan Publication.

Kale, Kishore Shantabai. 2000. *Against All Odds*. Translated by Sandhya Pandey. New Delhi: Penguin.

Limbale, Sharankumar. 2003. *The Outcaste: Akkarmashi*. Translated by Santosh Bhoomkar. Introduction by G N Devy. New Delhi: Oxford University Press.

Macwan, Joseph. 2004. *The Stepchild*. Translated by Rita Kothari. New Delhi: Oxford University Press.

Mane, Laxman. 1997. *Upara: An Outsider*. Translated by A K Kamat. New Delhi: Sahitya Akademi.

Moon, Vasant. 2001. *Growin Up Untouchable in India*. Translated by Gail Omvedt. Introduction and notes by Eleanor Zelliot. Blue Ridge Summit, PA: Rowman and Littlefield and New Delhi: Sage.

Pawar, Urmila. 1998. 'Amhihi Itihas Ghadawala.' Interview and two short stories. Mumbai: SPARROW (Sound and Pictures Archives for Research on Women).

———. 2001. 'Chauthi Bhint.' Translated by Gail Omvedt. Introduction by Eleanor Zelliot. *Manushi* 122 (January–February): 23–31.

Valmiki, Om Prakash. 2003. *Joothan: A Dalit's Life*. Translated by Arun Prabha Mukherjee. Kolkata: Samya and New York: Columbia University Press.

B. ANTHOLOGIES, COLLECTIONS, SPECIAL ISSUES

Anand, Mulk Raj, and Eleanor Zelliot, eds. 1992. *An Anthology of Dalit Literature (Poems)*. New Delhi: Gyan Publishing House.

Dangle, Arjun, ed. 1992. *Poisoned Bread: Translations from Marathi Dalit Literature*. Hyderabad: Orient Longman.

Dangle, Arjun, ed. [1992] 1994. *A Corpse in the Well: Translations from Modern Marathi Dalit Autobiographies*. Hyderabad: Orient Longman.

Devy, G N, ed. 2002. *Painted Words: An Anthology of Tribal Literature*. New Delhi: Penguin.

Joshi, Barabara R, ed. 1986. *Untouchable! Voices of the Dalit Liberation Movement*. London: Zed Books and Minority Rights Group.

Indian Literature 159, no. 47: 1 (January–February 1994). An overview of Gujarati Dalit Literature by K M Sherrif; a life sketch by Joseph Macwan; poems from Gujarati by Joseph Macwan, Muhammed Ishaq Sheikh, Jayant Parmar, Sanker Painter, Praveen Gadvi, Narsingh Ujamba, Yashvant Vaghela, Manal Rathod, Kisan Sosa and Raju

Solanki; short stories by Malhukant Kalpit, Naikal Gangera, Pathik Parmar, Mohan Parmar, Dalpat Chauhan and Harish Mangalam; interview with Mangalam.

Indian Literature 193, no. 43: 5 (September–October 1999). Issue on Tamil Dalit literature. Critical essays by K Satchidanandan on Kannada and Venkat Swaminathan on Telugu; poetry by Ila Murugu, Imayam and Palamalai; short stories by Bama, Perumal Murugan, Abhimaani, Vizhi. Paa. Idayavendan, Sundara Pandian, Unjai Rajan and Paavannan; essays by Imayam, Cho Dharman, Perumal Murugan and Bama.

Indian Literature 201, no. 45: 1 (January–February 2001). Tamil Dalit Fiction. Excerpts from novels by Imayam, Sivakami, Cho Dharman and Poomani.

Journal of South Asian Literature 17: 1 (1982). A Marathi Sampler. Stories by Shankarrao Kharat and Baburao Bagul; poems by Namdeo Dhasal, Daya Pawar and Trymbak Sapkale; critical essay on Namdeo Dhasal by Dilip Chitre.

Vagartha 12 (January 1976). Special Issue on Dalit Literature. Translations of Shankarrao Kharat, Baburao Bagul, Waman Nimbalkar and Daya Pawar.

C. CRITICISM

Anand, J H. 1995. 'Dalit Literature is the Literature of Protest.' In Bhagwan Das and James Massey, eds., *Dalit Solidarity*. New Delhi: ISPCK. 177–184.

Anand, S. 2003. *Touchable Tales: Publishing and Reading Dalit Literature*. Pondicherry: Navayana.

Biswas, Achintya. 1995. 'Bengali Dalit Poetry: Past and Now.' In Bhagwan Das and James Massey, eds., *Dalit Solidarity*. New Delhi: ISPCK. 190–200.

Challapalli, Swaroopa Rani. 1998. 'Dalit Women's Writing in Telugu.' *Economic and Political Weekly* (25 April 1998): 21–24.

Deo, Veena. 1996. 'Dalit Literature in Marathi.' In Nalini Natarajan, ed., *Handbook of Twentieth-Century Literature of India*. Westport, CT: Greenwood Press. 363–381.

Dewanji, Malay. 1994. *Dalit Literature—Quest for Dalit Liberation*. Bangalore: Christian Institute for the Study of Religion and Society.

Dharwadker, Vinay. 1994. 'Dalit Poetry in Marathi.' *World Literature Today* 68: 2 (spring): 319–324.

Gokhale-Turner, Jayashree. 1981. 'Bhakti or Vidroha: Continuity and Change in Dalit Literature.' *Journal of Asian and African Studies* 15: 1–2 (1980): 29–40. Reprinted in Jayant Lele, ed., *Tradition and Modernity in Bhakti Movements.* Leiden: EJ Brill.

Hovell, Laurie. 1991. 'Namdeo Dhasal: Poet and Panther.' *Bulletin of Concerned Asian Scholars* 23: 2 (1991): 77–83.

Jain, Jasbir. 2002. 'Dalit Women's Autobiographies: A Counter Discourse.' In Jasbir Jain, *Writing Women Across Cultures.* Jaipur and New Delhi: Rawat Publications. 282–293.

Joshi, Svati. 1990. 'Forging an Epistemology of Resistance: Dalit Writing in Gujarati.' *The Book Review* 143 (May–June): 32–33.

Kumar, Raj. 1995. 'Oriya Dalit Literature: A Historical Perspective.' *The Fourth World* 2 (October): 91–111.

Lal, Chaman. 1998. 'Dalit Trend in Punjabi Literature.' *Indian Literature* 185. no. 42: 3 (May–June): 13–17.

Lele, Jayant and Rajendra Singh. 1987. 'Language and Literature of Dalits and Sants: Some Missed Opportunities.' In Iqbal Narain and Lothar Lutze, eds., *Literature, Social Consciousness and Polity.* New Delhi: Manohar. 28–60.

Mukherjee, Arun. 1998. 'The Emergence of Dalit Writing.' In Arun Mukherjee, *Postcolonialism: My Living.* Toronto: TSAR. 41–51.

———. 1998. 'Facing the Interrogations of Dalit Writing.' In Arun Mukherjee, *Postcolonialism: My Living.* Toronto: TSAR. 52–64.

———. 1998. 'The Exclusions of Postcolonial Theory and Mulk Raj Anand's *Untouchable*: A Case Study.' In Arun Mukherjee, *Postcolonialism: My Living.* Toronto: TSAR. 133–151.

Murlidhar, T. 1996. 'Exhibiting Wounds: Dalit Self-Consciousness in Telugu Poetry.' *New Quest* 118 (July–August): 213–216.

Nagaraj, D R. 1993. *The Flaming Feet: A Study of the Dalit Movement in India.* Bangalore: South Forum Press.

———. 1994. 'From Political Rage to Cultural Affirmation: Notes on the Kannada Dalit Poet-Activist Siddalingaiah.' *India International Centre Quarterly* (winter).

Narasaiah, G Lakshmi. 1999. *The Essence of Dalit Poetry: A Socio-Philosophic Study of Telugu Dalit Poetry.* Hyderabad: Dalit Sena Publications.

Pandian, M S S. 1998. 'On a Dalit Woman's Testimonio.' *Seminar* 471 (November): 53–56.

———. 1998. 'Stepping Outside History? New Dalit Writings from Tamil Nadu.' In Partha Chaterjee, ed., *Wages of Freedom: Fifty Years of the Indian Nation-State.* New Delhi: Oxford University Press.

Punalekar, S P. 2001. 'Dalit Literature and Dalit Identity.' In Ghanshyam Shah, ed., *Dalit Identity and Politics.* New Delhi: Sage. 216–241.

———. 1997. 'Sociology of Dalit Autobiography.' In Ghanshyam Shah, ed., *Social Transformation in India: Essays in Honour of Professor I.P. Desai.* Vol. 2. Jaipur: Rawat Publications. 370–396.

Rentala, Kalpana. 2000. 'Contemporary Telugu Literature Survey: State of the Art.' (Including an extensive questionnaire). *Indian Literature* 200, no. 44: 6 (November–December).

Satyanarayana, A. 1994. 'Dalit Protest Literature in Telugu: A Historical Perspective.' *Economic and Political Weekly* 30: 3 (21 January): 171–175.

Tharakam, Bojja, ed. 1994. *First All India Dalit Writers Conference: A Commemorative Volume.* Hyderabad: Dr B R Ambedkar Memorial Trust.

Thorat, Vimal. 1996. 'Social Movement and Literary Consciousness: A Comparative Study of Hindi and Dalit Poetry in the Sixties.' Translated by Raj Kumar and Eleanor Zelliot. *The Fourth World* 3 (April): 58–64.

Zelliot, Eleanor. 2000. 'Sant Sahitya and Dalit Movements.' In Meera Kosambi, ed., *Intersections: Socio-cultural Trends in Maharashtra.* Hyderabad: Orient Longman.

———. 1996. 'Stri Dalit Sahitya: The New Voice of Women Poets.' In Anne Feldhaus, ed., *Images of Women in Maharashtrian Literature and Religion.* Albany: State University of New York Press. 65–93.

D. GENERAL

Ilaiah, Kancha. 1996. *Why I Am Not a Hindu: A Sudra Critique of Hindutva Philosophy, Culture and Political Economy.* Calcutta: Samya.

Jogdand, P G, ed. 1995. *Dalit Women: Issues and Perspectives.* New Delhi: Gyan Publishing House with University of Poona.

Omvedt, Gail. 1994. *Dalits and the Democratic Revolution: Dr. Ambedkar and the Dalit Movement in Colonial India.* New Delhi: Sage Publications.

———. [1995] 1996. *Dalit Visions.* Tracts for the Times/8. Hyderabad: Orient Longman.

Radhakrishna, Meena. 2002. *Dishonoured by History*. Hyderabad: Orient Longman.

Thirumaavalavan, Thol. 2003. *Talisman: Extreme Emotions of Dalit Liberation*. Kolkata. Samya.

Yadav, KC, ed. 2000. *From Periphery to Centre Stage: Ambedkar, Ambedkarism and Dalit Future*. New Delhi: Manohar.

Dalit Literature from Orient Longman

A Corpse in the Well: Translations from Modern Marathi Dalit Autobiographies

DANGLE, ARJUN (ed.)

A selection from the famous anthology Poisoned Bread

This book follows a literary form marked by a great quantity of writing equally matched by its quality. The autobiographies in this first English collection depict varying facets of Dalit life: the struggle for survival; the man–women relationship; an existence crushed under the wheels of village life; the experiencing of humiliation and atrocities; at times, abject submission and at other times, rebellion.

81 250 0269 3   74pp   Rs 45.00

Homeless in my Land: Translations from Modern Marathi Dalit Short Stories

DANGLE, ARJUN (ed.)

A selection from the famous anthology Poisoned Bread

The short stories in this first English anthology forcefully convey the 'differentness' of Dalit literature. The protagonists of these stories are shown struggling for survival at their different levels – confronting casteisms, limitations, abject poverty, misery and brutality – and fighting a brave battle.

81 250 0271 5   78pp   Rs 45.00

No Entry for the New Sun: Translations from Modern Marathi Dalit Poetry

DANGLE, ARJUN (ed.)

A selection from the famous anthology Poisoned Bread

The poets, presented here in English translation, are some of the most prominent figures in Marathi Dalit poetry. Their impassioned cry against subjugation, humiliation and atrocities, and their intoxicated singing of the dawn of a new life, are what this first English anthology of Dalit poetry is all about.

81 250 0270 7   84pp   Rs 45.00

Poisoned Bread: Translations from Modern Marathi Dalit Literature

DANGLE, ARJUN (ed.)

Silenced for centuries by caste prejudice and social oppression, the Dalits of Maharashtra (formerly called 'untouchables') have only in the last forty years found a powerful voice through Marathi literature. The revolutionary social movement launched by Dr Ambedkar was paralleled by a wave of writing that exploded in poetry, prose, fiction and autobiography which was shocking in its exposition. The writers – more than eighty of them – presented here, are some of the most prominent figures in Marathi Dalit literature.

0 86311 254 4   328pp   Rs 300.00

Chakra

DALVI, JAYAWANT

Translated from the Marathi by Gauri Deshpande

Life in Bombay's streets and slums forms the grim background to this novel, translated from Marathi. It won the author three literary awards.

0 86311 374 5   104pp   Rs 75.00

Dalit Visions (Tracts for the Times)

Omvedt, Gail

This book looks at alternative traditions nurtured within Dalit movements, which have questioned this method of looking at Indian society and its history. While seeking to understand the varied Dalit visions that have tried to alter the terms of the dominant order, this persuades us to reconsider our ideas and understand the visions which seek to change the world in which the Dalits live.

81 250 0636 2   110pp   Rs 75.00